The Untamed Garden

A REVEALING LOOK AT
our LOVE AFFAIR WITH PLANTS

SONIA DAY

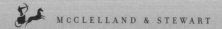 MCCLELLAND & STEWART

Library and Archives Canada Cataloguing in Publication

Day, Sonia
The untamed garden : a revealing look at our love affair with plants / Sonia Day.

ISBN 978-0-7710-2505-1

Gardens—History. 2. Gardening—History. I. Title.

SB451.D39 2011   712'.09   C2011-902200-1

Published simultaneously in the United States of America by McClelland & Stewart Ltd.,
P.O. Box 1030, Plattsburgh, New York 12901

Library of Congress Control Number: 2011925613

We acknowledge the financial support of the Government of Canada through the Book Publishing
Industry Development Program and that of the Government of Ontario through the Ontario
Media Development Corporation's Ontario Book Initiative. We further acknowledge the support
of the Canada Council for the Arts and the Ontario Arts Council for our publishing program.

Typeset in Filosofia by M&S, Toronto
Printed and bound in China

McClelland & Stewart Ltd.
75 Sherbourne Street
Toronto, Ontario M5A 2P9
www.mcclelland.com

1 2 3 4 5   15 14 13 12 11

For Carol, who has always loved the naughty bits

———

In memory of my gardener dad, Tom Day,
who fell in love with a night-blooming cereus

How can one help

shivering with delight

when one's hot fingers

close around the stem

of a live flower?

COLETTE

Contents

INTRODUCTION

It's a humid night in the tropics. The air is heavy and sweet, like honey. The only sound, apart from the cicadas' high-pitched whine, is the clink-clink of ice cubes as we sit on the patio, sipping rum and Coke, reading. And waiting.

Suddenly, at around ten, a Volkswagen Beetle chugs into the driveway. The editor of the local newspaper leaps out, breathless. He's wearing a creased Hawaiian shirt with damp patches in the armpits. There's a Pentax in his hand. "Sorry I'm late, Tom," he calls out. "Deadlines, you know. Has it happened yet?"

"Oh no," says my father, chuckling. "Come in, Paul. Want a rum? We'll probably have to wait all night."

And we very nearly did. The event that our perspiring journalist friend rushed over to witness, back when I was barely nineteen, finally started after midnight. And I have never forgotten the experience.

The proof of what happened—a faded newspaper clipping—lies now, tucked in a drawer, at my home in rural Ontario. I take it out now and then and remember. It shows the photo Paul took on that sultry August night in the Bahamas so many years ago. My proud dad stands grinning like a Cheshire cat as he shows off his "lady"—a night-blooming cereus in full lusty bloom, the flower's creamy petals shining like silky, see-through lingerie. It was the first time that the cereus had bloomed for Dad. And the thrill was short-lived. Almost as fleeting as a kiss. His precious flower withered and crumpled—as cereus do—only a few hours later. Yet how happy she made us, his queen of the night. How sweetly she smelled. How her golden stamens sparkled in the tropical dawn. I still recall almost every detail of my brief encounter with her.

Plants are like that. They can leave you with thrilling memories that last a lifetime. Subliminally or not, I think my father's passion for his cereus made me want to become a gardener myself. And as I got older and started growing things like he did, I became even more aware that plants and flowers aren't simply pretty things to look at. They also have the ability to arouse our senses. They can be incredibly exciting—and erotic.

In the past, many cultures exulted in this glorious quality. They enjoyed an intimate relationship with their plants and flowers and celebrated their sexuality in a variety of colourful ways.

Yet we don't. Not anymore. And that's too bad, because if more people were aware of the sensual aura of plants, perhaps gardening wouldn't be dismissed—as it increasingly is—as a pursuit enjoyed only by old codgers who have nothing better to do than blather on about their begonias and beefsteak tomatoes.

The truth is, the plant world is drenched in sex. Passionate, urgent, unabashed sex. Buds swell suggestively. Phallic stalks thrust skywards. Enticing orifices and lolling tongues invite probing. Labia-like petals fold back to reveal tiny clitoral appendages. There are twirly black bits at the centre of flowers, as erotically charged as pubic hair. Honeyed nectar drips from the ends of long wiggly protuberances. Pornographic couplings take place. And ah, those seductive scents, like the one wafting from my father's cereus.

The graphic displays and perfumes are of course aimed at the insects, birds, and animals that play a role in pollinating plants, but there's nothing to stop us from enjoying them too. So why don't we?

It's surprising, really. Although Eros is never far removed from our pruners and planting schemes, most gardeners rarely acknowledge the fact. You might even describe sex as gardening's dirty little secret, kept neatly tucked away, under the plant catalogues stacked on the front porch. Out of sight and—mostly—out of mind.

Yet in the twenty-first century, when just about anything goes, prissy perceptions about plants are surely an anachronism. It's time to let them go, to bring some excitement back into the pleasure of growing things. That's why I wrote this book—to encourage people to start celebrating the wild, sexy side of Mother Nature as humans once did, because it's been shunted aside and forgotten for far too long.

The same conclusion might strike you after dipping into these pages. And who knows? Like my dad, you might even wind up falling in love.

SONIA DAY

The Untamed Garden

Lilium candidum.

Victor.

INNOCENCE

THE MADONNA LILY
The purest flower in the world

Ever wondered where the expression that a virgin has been "deflowered" comes from?

The answer lies in prudish attitudes to the facts of life, which persisted—amazingly—for thousands of years.

It may sound laughable today, but people actually once clung to the belief that plants were somehow different from the rest of us. That is, they didn't have sex in order to reproduce themselves. Instead, the botanical world was a totally pure and innocent place, a sort of fantasy land, in fact. Thus a girl who lost her virginity was said to have been deflowered because she no longer possessed the sexless quality of a flower. Yes, pretty weird

stuff. Yet plants were imbued with this strange ideal for a surprisingly long time—well into the twentieth century—and by a
surprisingly diverse group of experts. Over the years, not one
philosopher, doctor, botanist, or naturalist saw fit to challenge
this belief—which seems odd, when you think about it.
Although their lives were dedicated to the pursuit of science,
these learned gents didn't ever bother to ask themselves a
couple of basic questions. One: if plants don't have sex with
each other, then how do they go about producing more plants?
And two: what are their seeds for?

The flower that best sums up this cockeyed attitude to nature
is the Madonna lily. Look closely at almost any early ecclesiastical
art that features the Virgin Mary—there's lots in churches and art
galleries throughout Italy and Spain—and
this lily, whose Latin name is *Lilium candi-*
dum, is likely to be included somewhere.
Early Christians regarded the flower as
sacred because the pristine white petals
symbolized Mary's spotless body, while its
clusters of golden stamens represented a soul gleaming with
heavenly light. In one famous painting, called the *Annunciation*,
which hangs in Florence's Uffizi Gallery, master artist Leonardo
da Vinci has even positioned a big spray of Madonna lilies smack
next to the nose of an angel, who is shown in profile. And they are

huge, these blooms. Suspended apparently in mid-air, they jump out at you. In choosing to depict the lilies so prominently, Leonardo clearly wanted us to notice their symbolism.

This painting shows the moment when the angel announces to Mary that she will give birth to the son of God—and his message is obvious. She is pure. But so is the white flower beside her.

FLOWERS *finally* GET A SEX LIFE

Pity Monsieur M. Pouyanne. This belief in the purity of plants got him into deep trouble. He was a Frenchman toiling as a judge advocate in steamy Algeria at the beginning of the twentieth century. But his passion was the study of nature, and one day he noticed something extraordinary happening to an orchid in his collection, called *Ophrys speculum*. A wasp landed on it, clung to one of its petals, and performed some energetic jerky movements—an act that looked suspiciously as if the wasp was trying to mate with the flower. Then he noticed that the centre of this orchid looked remarkably like the female version of the same wasp. So in 1916, he wrote an article for the *Journal of the National Horticultural Society of France* suggesting that this activity indeed might be mating and that the orchid actually mimicked the appearance of the female wasp in order to "achieve some goal."

Pouyanne's prose was mild, the typical dry fodder of horticultural journals. Mindful of the prevailing attitudes of the day
(and that, as an amateur naturalist, he wouldn't be regarded as
an expert), he did not go so far as to propose that the orchid was
trying to trick the wasp into collecting pollen on its body so that
when it flew away to another orchid, the grains would get carried
along too and be transferred to the sexual apparatus of the second
orchid, thereby helping pollination to take place. No, he was much
more cautious than that. Even so, the French judge's words provoked a firestorm. Dirty old man!
howled the academic establish-
ment. What a ridiculous suggestion, shrieked botanists. How could
a learned journal print such rubbish, because plants don't—repeat,
don't—have sexual organs. Even Charles Darwin, granddaddy of
evolution, huffed that he "could not possibly conjecture" what
the bee's frantic jigging up and down on the orchid was all about.

The lily is all in white, like a saint,
And so is no mate for me.

THOMAS HOOD, "FLOWERS"

Yet the critics couldn't really be written off as silly, self-
important fools. They were only doing what had been done for
centuries. Over and over again. Ad nauseam. Long before
Pouyanne's controversial opinion piece, luminaries were getting their knuckles rapped for theorizing that plants required a
sexual act to reproduce themselves. One expert who took a lot
of heat in this regard was Swedish botanist Carl Linnaeus. After

studying stamens (which he concluded were the male part of the flower) and pistils (their female counterpart), he devised a new system of classifying plants according to the number and arrangement of their reproductive organs. In his manuscripts, Linnaeus also, in a very daring move, often attributed human attitudes and behaviour to plants' sexual characteristics. One group he described, for instance, as "openly celebrating marriage in a way that is obvious to all" (in other words, their sexual organs were noticeably prominent in their flowers). In his mania to classify everything, Linnaeus even categorized his comely young wife, Sara, as his "monandrian lily"—because the flower signified virginity and "monandrian" meant "having only one man."

But Linnaeus wasn't taken seriously either. Although this eminently sensible botanist came up with a satisfactory system of naming and classifying plants that (despite a few quibbles) is still in use today, he went to his grave (at the age of seventy in 1778) worried sick about the "divine retaliation" that was in store for him. The reason? The critics called his theories about plant sex "obscene" and "offensive to public decency."

don't GIVE YOUR LOVE A PETUNIA

Sex between plants was a taboo topic when Linnaeus lived. Yet human sex didn't fare much better. If you fell in love back then,

you couldn't say so. Dear me, no. It just wasn't done to acknowledge sexual urges or express feelings openly. Thus the language
of flowers was born. This idea of using plants to send secret mes-
sages started with the flower-loving
Turks (who were the first people to
cultivate tulips), but later caught on
in Europe—and understandably so.
What could be more perfect than
sending someone a beautiful flower—
or a bunch of flowers—and in doing
so discreetly revealing exactly what
was on your mind?

The French and English became
the biggest fans of this new, novelty
language. During the nineteenth
century, the meanings of individual
flowers were the subject of spicy
gossip circulating in salons and
drawing rooms on both sides of the
Channel. If a certain lady received a
bouquet from a certain gentleman, the ladies in her circle
would examine the blooms contained in that bouquet in
minute detail in order to find clues as to his intentions.
Several books were published detailing exactly what

A Few Flowers and Their Meanings

CARNATION (PINK): I'll never forget you
CARNATION (WHITE): Sweet and lovely, innocence
HYACINTH (PINK): I am sorry, please forgive me
HYACINTH (WHITE): Loveliness, I'll pray for you
ORANGE BLOSSOM: Innocence, eternal love, marriage
LILY (ORANGE): Hatred
LILY (WHITE): Virginity, purity
LILY OF THE VALLEY (ALWAYS WHITE): Tears of the Virgin Mary
ROSE (CORAL): Desire
ROSE (WHITE): Innocence, secrecy

to look for, and hundreds of flowers (plus a few foliage plants) wound up with symbolic meanings. Virtually all of them concern some aspect of love. In fact, think of any vaguely amorous emotion (of the printable kind) and you can probably come up with a flower that fits. A pansy, for instance, says "You are in my thoughts," while a sunflower expresses "loyalty." If you are angry at someone, there's the petunia (it means "resentment" or "anger"), while larkspur says "You are fickle." The list goes on and on.

Colours also played an important role in determining what sentiment was ascribed to certain flowers. White flowers, for instance, almost invariably got linked (like the Madonna lily in Leonardo's painting) to that valued ideal, innocence. Nowadays, florists and wedding planners seem to be the only ones who take these coded meanings seriously, usually when they're putting together bridal bouquets and table decorations for wedding receptions. Yet even a hundred years ago, the language of flowers was a bona fide method used by both sexes to express themselves.

the FLOWER that STIRRED THE ENVY of VENUS

There are many colourful myths about Madonna lilies. That's because *Lilium candidum* is believed to be the world's oldest "domesticated" flower (meaning that it was the first to be cultivated). The name signifies "dazzling whiteness" in Latin, and both the Christian and Jewish religions, captivated by this quality, imbued the flower with its virginal aura. Yet much earlier, it was regarded as anything but chaste. The flower's sheer voluptuousness—big, showy blooms in silky, iridescent white, shaped like horns and embellished with twirly gold threads—came through loud and clear. In fact, for some cultures, the Madonna lily was a bit of a strumpet.

Love Potion Number 1

If your relationship is platonic, but you'd like it to go further, give a bouquet of white lilies combined with red roses. The lilies signify innocence, the roses love and desire.
INSTRUCTIONS ON A FLORIST'S WEB SITE

The Romans, predictably, took this ribald view. They linked the white lily to Venus, goddess of love. For them, the flower symbolized "lustful ardour," not purity, and in one of their salacious stories, Venus rose from seafoam and encountered a lily whose pristine petals and beauty made her insanely jealous. So she ordered a "huge and monstrous pistil" to spring up in the centre of this flower, which she hoped would encourage horny satyrs to come galloping over and have their carnal way with the lily. And the Romans certainly made a good point about those pistils. Very long and prominent they are in lilies, while the stamens that surround them develop in the same way. Both protuberances wave themselves around provocatively, especially on a windy day, in a message that's certainly—to the observant eye—more come-hither than innocent. And this apparent lewdness of lilies (behaviour they adopt simply to pollinate themselves) eventually got noticed by the Victorians, who were finally waking up to the fact that the long-held belief in the "innocence" of plants was nothing but a bunch of hooey. In fact, their horrified clergy decided that the flowers could look pretty suggestive. So they routinely removed the stamens and pistils from white lily blooms displayed on church altars on the grounds that such "overt symbols of sexuality" might move the congregation to think impure thoughts. Tut-tut.

Before the Romans, one Greek legend told a tale of marital strife involving the white lily. In theirs, Zeus fathered a child with a mortal called Alcerne and then saddled his missus, Hera, with the job of breastfeeding the babe. Furious with him, she ripped the child from her breast, and her milk splattered across the heavens, forming the Milky Way. A few drops also plummeted to earth. Where they landed, the white lily popped up.

Then multiplied like crazy, it seems. Today, you can see interpretations of this lily everywhere—on Assyrian carvings,

Egyptian tombs, thousand-year-old Greek murals, you name it. Visit museums in Crete displaying art from the Minoan era and it's the most-used floral emblem you'll encounter. The white lily is also popular in China (where it means "forever in love"), and the Old and New Testaments of the Bible mention it no less than fourteen times—more often than any other flower.

"Consider the lilies of the field." Who isn't familiar with this simple but evocative statement from the Bible? It's become so well known, a movie that won Sidney Poitier an Academy Award even filched part of the line to use as a title. Although there is some doubt now that *Lilium candidum* grew in the Holy Land at all (the expression "lilies of the field" may have simply been used to describe all kinds of flowers), Christians believe these words were spoken by Jesus Christ, while Jews link the flower to the Star of David (when fully open, the bloom has a similar star-like shape). And whether you subscribe to those views or not, this flower is certainly a joy to behold—a bright, shining, uplifting creation that perhaps sprang into existence to remind us just how precious and heavenly our world is.

MAKE-BELIEVE MADONNAS

As spiritual as the Madonna lily looks, you're unlikely to find her on sale at Easter. The flower that's imbued with so much religious symbolism is unfortunately difficult to grow. So over the years, she has been displaced by the *Lilium longiflorum,* an upstart look-alike import from Japan. *L. longiflorum* is the lily that's now raised by the millions in greenhouses, then shipped off—their plastic pots wrapped in shiny green foil, half a dozen bullet-shaped buds ready to burst open on each tall, straight stem—to sell at supermarkets and garden centres everywhere in the weeks leading up to Good Friday. And although it's now common—and remarkably cheap—and thus taken for granted, this lily was once highly prized and very expensive. Bear that in mind if you buy a *L. longiflorum* to give to your mom on Easter Sunday. Treat it with respect.

Easter morn with lilies fair
Fills the church with perfumes rare,
As their clouds of incense rise,
Sweetest offerings to the skies.
Stately lilies pure and white
Flooding darkness with their light . . .

LOUISE LEWIN MATTHEWS, "EASTER MORN"

MORBID MADONNAS

The most famous lilies in the world have a shady side. Along with innocence and purity, they are associated with death, as are many white flowers. Often used at funerals (two wreaths adorned the coffin of Princess Diana as it travelled through the streets of London—one of white lilies, the other of white roses), the white lily is subject to some long-established superstitions. In Britain, for instance, some people still believe that you must never bring them inside the home or somebody who lives there will die.

During the Second World War, this superstition puzzled some Chinese residents of Malaysia who were turned away from military hospitals when they showed up carrying bouquets of *Lilium longiflorum* to cheer up wounded servicemen. And although British gardeners have always been fond of white flowers (Vita Sackville-West's White Garden at Sissinghurst is one example of the veneration accorded to this hue), some old-timers wouldn't dream of picking the pristine lilies that grow in their flower beds and then arranging them indoors, in a vase. Residents of rural England once blamed the white lily for meddling in matrimonial matters too. White lilies shouldn't come into a house where a young unmarried girl lived, one superstition went, because then she would never find herself a husband.

Yet this flower of such contradictory symbolism did, it seems, serve one practical purpose. In bygone days, its petals, steeped in brandy, were placed on cuts, scratches, and bruises and reportedly healed these wounds "like a miracle."

A miracle? Perhaps there *is* something, after all, to the religious fervour that surrounds this symbol of goodness and purity.

FLIRTATION

THE PEONY

The floppy show-off that everyone adores

The language of flowers ladies (who were around in the 1800s) got peonies wrong—hopelessly wrong. They decided that these plants denoted "bashfulness," because of a Greek myth about mischievous cherubs hiding themselves in the flowers' voluminous petals.

Okay, it's a cute image. But bashful? You've got to be kidding. No one in their right mind would describe peonies that way. Flashy, yes. And flirty. And flamboyant. And flouncy. And flagrant. And . . . A trowelful of adjectives beginning with an *f* comes immediately to mind when picturing how these flowers look, yet "bashful" doesn't figure in the equation. Not at all.

Those upper-class females who sat around in their hoop skirts, dreaming up symbols for flowers, had perhaps got into the laudanum by the time they'd moved down the alphabet to peonies. So they goofed.

Because far from being shy and retiring, these flowers are surely among the most shameless exhibitionists ever created by Mother Nature. In reality, with their blowsy, D-cup blooms strutting atop those precarious chicken-leg stems they are (to modern eyes at least) the Dolly Partons of the garden. Like the country singer, they can come across as a tad vulgar and over the top, yet that's the secret of their indefatigable charm too. People seem to love Dolly's outrageous sense of chutzpah and it's surely the same with peonies—which are, when you think about it, ridiculous, exasperating, and pointless flowers, because they often collapse at the drop of a hat. Those thin stems never seem to be able to prop up the too-weighty blooms for very long, even with the newer, less top-heavy single varieties, and the mess they leave behind can severely test our patience. Yet, despite this defect, you will rarely meet anyone who dislikes peonies. On the contrary. To most gardeners, they are heaven-sent objects of adoration.

Why? Just take a look at a big clump of peonies, resplendent with blooms, on a June day. Even the most abundant of roses pale beside prolific peonies. Their very extravagance is surely unmatched by anything else we grow—so many opulent petals on each huge flower head, and, often, such an amazing number of flower heads, all popping open from their odd gobstopper buds at once. Reliably as clockwork every year too, with no prodding at all from us. (Hard winters don't—what bliss!—faze their hulking great roots. Nor do they demand fussing with fertilizers.) Then bend over a bloom. Breathe in deeply. Their scents can be delicious—delicate, light, sweet, yet strong enough to waft all over the garden—and their colours are equally mouthwatering. Froths of pure white, creamy vanilla or lemon, sugary pink shot through with ripples of raspberry, tangerine touched with a tease of orange, luminous cherry red, and a deep, delicious plum that positively shimmers. Ornamented at their centres with tangles of twirly, golden threads, our volup-tuous peonies float atop their handsome dark green foliage like luscious cut-open peaches and dishes of delec-table ice cream. They look almost good enough to eat.

Yet like any delicious treat, the sensory pleasure is tantalizingly short, over almost as soon as it starts. Peony petals start drop-ping within a week, often less. And inevitably, infuriatingly, a rain or wind storm will roll in when the blooms are going full blast, causing the stems underneath to immediately collapse in an untidy heap, transforming our objects of worship into wads of wet Kleenex, nasty and slippery, piling up on the garden path. If you're quick enough, you can rush around like crazy with a pair of secateurs, frantically cutting blooms off to bring them indoors before the full force of the rain or wind wreaks this destruction. (And it's worth doing, because peonies make the most elegant and classy cut flowers in the world.) But usually, we're too late. Once the realization hits that the show's over for another year, all that's left to do is sigh, recall how breathtakingly beautiful Mother Nature's short burst of munificence was, then sweep up the heaps of sodden petals, hoping, a bit grimly, perhaps, for drier, calmer days next June.

There is one peony lover, bewitched by their spell, who, loath to leave them for even a few hours, makes the rounds of her garden every night with a lantern. [And she] often rises to listen to the birds and see her peonies at dawn.

ALICE HARDING, *The Peony*

But who would be without peonies? Not many northern gardeners, if they're familiar with their spectacular allure and have the space to grow them. (They require lots of sun, an open aspect, and good drainage.) This is, after all, a love affair that has lasted for thousands of years.

the HEALING POWER *of* PEONIES

These flowers unquestionably inspire obsessive fits of passion in their owners. Sooner or later, almost everyone who owns one peony clump wants to make space for another. Even so, in European culture, peonies don't have the racy history of roses and orchids and are usually associated with the ability to heal. The word "peony" comes from the Greek god Paeon. His is a complicated and confusing myth (like so many). He is said to have extracted a milky white liquid from peony roots and used it to cure Pluto, who'd got into a spat with Hercules and wound up being shot in the shoulder with an arrow. But then Aesculapius leaps into the story. This gent with the tongue-twisting name was the god of medicine and not at all happy about said miracle cure. Feeling profession-ally threatened, he decided to kill Paeon off. So Pluto intervened and turned poor Paeon into a flower that people would admire and praise forever. To this day, we use the word "paean" to describe a laudatory statement or song about someone or something.

A more titillating telling of this legend skips the healing aspect. Instead, the heroine is Paeonia, a hot-to-trot nymph who flirts with Apollo, arousing the ire of Aphrodite. One day this goddess catches the couple *in flagrante delicto* and Paeonia blushes so deeply, Aphrodite turns her into a rosy red peony.

Myths aside, the medicinal mythology surrounding peonies kept spreading like outbreaks of the measles. Pliny the Elder, who was around in AD 77 (and was asphyxiated at Pompeii when Vesuvius erupted), claimed that no fewer than twenty "diseases of the body" could be cured by eating peony roots and seeds. He counselled digging up the plants at night and soaking the seeds

Pæonia officinalis

in red wine as a potion to "heal the uterus" of whatever ailed it. The roots were preferred to "relieve all pains of the belly, open the bowels, cure tetanus and prevent nightmares"— beliefs that persisted in Europe well into the nineteenth century. Children in England wore necklaces made from the roots to prevent convulsions and assist teething woes. Epilepsy and snake bites were other ills that received the root treatment.

Some creepy superstitions also surrounded peonies. One was that, if you count an odd number of blooms on a peony plant, someone in your household will die within a year. Fortunately, it's not true.

the SECRET TO HOLDING *an* EMPEROR'S LOVE

For healing purposes, Europeans used herbaceous peonies—
that is, large perennials that have tuberous roots and bushy
foliage that dies down to the ground every winter. But much
earlier, in China, people were falling head over heels in love with
another member of this plant family: the tree
peony *P. suffruticosa*. The name is actually a bit
of a misnomer, because these aren't trees at
all, but big, shrubby plants that can reach a
height of six feet or more and that have hard,
twiggy stems to support their busty blooms
(although these are still inclined to flop). The
Chinese call the plants *moutan*. As beautifully bedecked as
herbaceous peonies, tree kinds usually cost more and sometimes sulk in North American gardens. (They react badly to
harsh winters, when whole branches or sections of the plant
will sometimes die off.) But what gives them a bit of an edge
over their European relatives is their symbolism. Tree peonies
are steeped in sex.

I'll whisper
as he sleeps
the sound
of white peony petals
falling

ANGELA LEUCK

That Victorian stuff about bashfulness? Forget it. To the
Chinese, the peony is—far more fittingly—a symbol of beauty,
romance, marriage, prosperity, and the magical lightheartedness

of youth. And with a catalogue of charms like that, titillating tid-bits crop up in Asian history as plentifully as the petals on a peony. One story concerns an early emperor of the Tang Dynasty, Sui Yangdi, whose favourite concubine, known as Yang Gui Fei, pos-sessed "extraordinary lovemaking skills." She is still celebrated as one of China's most desirable women. Apparently, Yang Gui Fei's principal tool of enticement was peonies. And how savvy she was, this cunning little seductress, filling her living quarters with big bouquets of the flowers, arranged in vases. She clearly knew a thing or two about their erotic possibilities.

Just for fun, take a page out of her creative book of love. Linger with someone special (preferably on a long sofa, piled with velvet and satin cushions) beside a vase of cut peonies. Inhale their glo-rious perfume first. Then watch together as one big blowsy bloom gradually opens itself wide, spreading its gold stamens apart, to reveal, often, a tight little orb at the centre of the flower. The sight is certainly erotically charged, and in a warm room, this blossom-ing of the flower's inner self happens quite quickly. There's more, too. After revealing her intimate parts, the bloom will start drop-ping her soft, overripe, skin-like petals, one by one, all over the floor, in a languid and lovely performance that's a perfect sequel to the energy of passion. Watching the petals glide to the ground inevitably prompts speculation about the emperor's lady love. Did she cleverly arrange for the cooling petals to land on their naked bodies while they lay intertwined, sweaty and exhausted, after satiating their lust? If so, it's hardly surprising that he stayed in love with her for years.

Love Potion Number 2

FENG SHUI FROLICS

Peonies figure strongly in this ancient Chinese tradition, now beloved by decorating divas everywhere. A few moves they recommend:

- For women: the chi peonies emit will attract wonderful partners. Keep a vase of the cut flowers in your living room or main family room.
- To reignite passion in a relationship, or to attract a new lustful lover into your life: display peonies either beside the main entrance of your home or in the southwest sector of the living room.
- For single men seeking a faithful woman to marry: place a mesmerizing peony in the southwest sector of your bedroom. This will stimulate Yin energy in the vicinity of your bed, and a loyal and lasting love will grow.

As the popularity of the flowers increased all over China, so did their association with sensuality, glamorous women, and the high life. Subsequent emperors presented favourite concubines with peony species that were named after them, and the peony image started cropping up as a subject in poetry, paintings, embroidery, and decorated porcelain. In Japan, however, the flower became a symbol associated with masculinity. To this day, some Japanese men get their bodies tattooed with intricate peony designs, inspired by early woodcuts, to signify a devil-may-care attitude to life.

Yet, as in Europe, peonies' power to heal came to the fore throughout Asia. And stayed. The roots of wild *P. suffruticosa* are still used in traditional Chinese medicine. Experiments are also being conducted to assess the roots' antimicrobial effect on two scourges of the modern world—the *E. coli* and *Staphylococcus* bacteria—but the research is not without its drawbacks. Only wild peonies appear to have medicinal value—nursery-propagated kinds don't deliver the same effect—and horticulturists worry that indiscriminate harvesting may make some species of the flower go the way of the dodo bird.

ADDING PEONIES *to the* STEWPOT

It happened in medieval England, when spices imported from
the Far East were so extremely expensive that people turned
to the flavouring possibilities of the homegrown peony instead.
Their seeds, which taste peppery, were used to spice up stews,
the roots got cooked as vegetables, and as late as 1747, Mrs.
Glasse's *The Art of Cookery* recommended "sticking cream
with peony kernels." In Kazakhstan, people made an equally
unpalatable-sounding gruel by boil-
ing the roots in water or milk, and
farther north, in ice-bound Siberia,
the roots of one species, *P. anomala,*
were dried, then simmered with meat

> Be careful if you take this
> flower into your house.
> The peony has a thousand lips.
>
> EVE ALEXANDRA, "GIRL"

during the wintertime, when fresh foodstuffs were scarce. The
Chinese, meanwhile, seemed to be having more fun. They
fermented the petals of tree peonies into a sweet and fragrant
liqueur called *moudan* wine. It is still sold in Heze, one of the
country's main centres for peony production. But nowhere, it
seems, has any culture hit on the idea of incorporating the
plant's luscious petals into a salad. Given their mouthwatering
colours, fragrance, and texture (not to mention their erotic
associations), it's surely time. Foodies, are you listening?

PASSIONATE PEONIES

The blooms of all peonies have an erotic quality that's evident in some of their names. A saucy sampling:

'Gay Paree': A mix of cherry, seashell pink, and white double petals. Showy enough to be kicking up her legs at the Folies Bergère.

'Molly the Witch': So named because her Latin name, *Paeonia mlokosetschii* (picked by Swedish botanist Linnaeus), is a nightmare to pronounce. Single golden petals, as shiny as silk. A favourite of peony fanciers. "Breathtaking, but like passion, it doesn't last long," laments one fan.

'Nymphe': Bowl-shaped, with masses of deep pink blossoms. A very old double variety that's a favourite of gardeners. Fragrance as fresh as a nymph cavorting in the woods.

'Petticoat Flounce': Tree type. Double white, pink-tinged petals with a tease of raspberry here and there. As sensually charged as a frilly Victorian petticoat.

'Pillow Talk': Fleshy, fluffy froths of rose-pink petals, tinged darker at their tips. Fragrant too. Beautiful enough to join bouts in the boudoir.

'Queen of Sheba': Delicious, deep magenta. Older variety. Blooms big and bosomy, like country queen Dolly Parton.

'Sarah Bernhardt': A confection of double pink petals, named after the actress who seduced French audiences at the turn of the twentieth century. Powerful perfume. A favourite of design diva Martha Stewart.

'Scarlett O'Hara': Appropriately scarlet petals. Lusty enough to be whisked upstairs and ravished by Clark Gable.

OTHER FLAUNTING FLORAS

Butterfly pea *Clitoria ternatea:* Oh boy. If ever a Latin name fitted, this one does. The flower of this plant looks so like a woman's private parts, it's embarrassing. A member of the pea family, this kind of *Clitoria* comes in several varieties, most notably bright blue, and is used a lot in hanging baskets, because it trails nicely. However, due to its marked resemblance to genitalia (turn the flowers upside down to get the full picture), it was once used in India to treat bedroom difficulties like infertility and erectile dysfunction. And aside from making us blush, the flower's in-your-face apparatus does serve a practical purpose. It lures male bees. They land on the large protruding lower lip, which provides space enough for a steady footing, then thrust their tongues deep into the sizable clitoris to reach nectar hidden inside the flower. The thrusting business is pretty frantic, too, according to Alec Bristow, author of *The Sex Life of Plants*, because curvaceous little *Clitoria* is partial to rough sex. She grips the bee hard, refusing to let him go until she's sure he's got himself thoroughly powdered in pollen (which he'll then obligingly transport to another flower). "It is a strenuous performance requiring considerable force," notes Bristow wryly, in a chapter of his book he calls "Bondage and Sadism."

Fall-flowering crocus *Colchichum autumnale*: Tiny, timid crocuses qualify as sexual exhibitionists? Well, yes, if they happen to be the late-blooming kind. With petals the colour of skin, these showgirls kick up their legs in most North American gardens late in the growing season, and their sassy performance is pure Las Vegas. The reason is timing. The tubular flowers of *Colchichum* pop out of the ground when everything else around them is fading away into the colours of fall. One minute, you're looking at a flower bed that's all muted browns and golds, and the next there's this startling explosion of pink flesh shouting, "Hey, you. Come over and look. We're summer's last burst of fun!" Strictly speaking, these late bloomers aren't related to the spring-flowering kind of crocus, even though they look like larger versions that have gulped a ton of steroids. One of their popular names is meadow saffron. However, over the years, the concupiscent appearance of *Colchichum* has given rise to other, more suggestive monikers. In England, people once called them "naked nannies." Appropriate? Only those who've actually seen a nanny without her clothes on (hopefully a youthful one) know for sure.

Flamingo flower *Anthurium*: This doesn't resemble the tropi-
cal bird at all, but instead looks mighty peculiar, with petals rather like plastic. Florists love *Anthurium*, though, because they stand out in a bouquet, and their phallic white centre spikes are certainly attention-getters. One female fan in Toronto tells the tale of buying a bunch of these flowers and carrying it home on the subway with her. "Every man who got into the subway car looked at the anthuriums and raised his eyebrows," she remembers with a laugh. "Then they kept looking hard at me."

Oriental poppy *Papaver orientale*: Think Bizet's Carmen, pranc-
ing around in a see-through scarlet skirt, driving Don José
mad with desire because he's noticed that she's not wearing
any panties. That's the Oriental poppy for you. Surely one of
the most erotic-looking flowers in the world, this kind of
poppy sports stamens that look like a bush of black pubic
hair, especially when they're starting to loosen up a little
and twist in the wind. And what a tease those little curls are,
peeping out from under the huge, transparent crepe-paper
petals. If you're going to grow these poppies, pick the blar-
ing red varieties—the bigger the better. They have the most
erotic fire power.

ROMANCE

THE ROSE
Ravishing—but not on Valentine's Day

What's the most "romantic" flower in the world? Easy. Even a macho guy who wouldn't be caught dead looking at plants in a garden knows the answer to that question. It's the rose.

We can credit St. Valentine for this level of awareness. He was a priest who got his head chopped off by the Pope back in AD 270 over a dispute about the right of soldiers to marry—and poor fellow, he probably never even knew what roses looked like. Yet every year, on the day of his death, males of all ages and from all walks of life now dutifully drop by a flower shop to pick up a bunch of the flowers that have become so indelibly associated with his name.

Giving roses—preferably red ones—to your girlfriend/wife/ Significant Other on February 14 is a rite of mid-winter. Sort of like eating turkey and pumpkin pie at Thanksgiving. And it's just something that you've gotta do, if you're a man. The slim bouquet may cost an arm and a leg (florists make more money during Valentine's week than the entire rest of the year) but guys-in-the-know don't let this significant date go by unheeded. Ignore it and you're likely to wind up sleeping on the sofa for a month.

Love Potion Number 3

When wild roses are blooming in the hedgerows, a handful of their petals, freshly gathered and placed beneath the bed, can be relied upon to make the woman willing . . .

CULPEPER'S COMPLETE HERBAL, SEVENTEENTH CENTURY

Yet what do these ridiculously expensive, long-stemmed florists' roses have to do with real romance? Truthfully, very little. Indeed, there is something so prissy, so stiff, so chaste, so utterly lifeless about their tightly furled buds—usually the required dozen in red—wrapped up and presented to a loved one in a coy cone of paper. Nuns in habits, not amorous encounters, come to mind. And that's hardly surprising. Because these are scentless, stand-ardized, cookie-cutter roses, raised in sweatshop greenhouses throughout Asia and South America and then shipped to cut flower markets located everywhere from Brussels to Beijing. Their blooms are bred to be identical in size, shape, and appearance. They get churned out by the millions, like shoes in a factory. Not exactly an auspicious beginning for flowers that are supposed to ignite wild nights of love.

But ah, the full-blown, genuine rose. Just head out into the garden and take a look at *her*.

real ROSES are RAVISHING

Disporting herself in a flower bed, petals flung wide open to the sun, wind, and rain, a full-blown, honest-to-goodness rose, sprung from the soil, is a far more seductive and appealing creature than those sexless mass-produced cut offerings men feel obligated to buy from florists every February.

Voluptuous. Sensual. Sometimes heavily perfumed. A conglomeration of curves, with the satiny feel of flesh or, on a dewy morning, moistened, ready-to-kiss lips. Altogether seductive to touch and gaze upon.

"Most roses show their sex organs as they fall open in the last wanton stages of bloom," points out writer Diane Ackerman in *Cultivating Delight*, a memoir about the lusty pleasures of her upstate New York garden. And it's true. The overt sexuality

HENDERSON'S "AURORA" COLLECTION of HARDY EVERBLOOMING ROSES

SOUVENIR DU PRES. CARNOT

WHITE MAMAN COCHET

SOUVENIR DE WOOTTON

PETER HENDERSON & CO. NEW YORK.

exhibited by these blooms has captivated everyone from Eros to D.H. Lawrence, author of one of the steamiest novels of the twentieth century. In *Lady Chatterley's Lover*, published in 1928 and promptly banned by many countries, Mellors the game-keeper enjoys a torrid tussle between the sheets with her lady-ship and then likens her golden skin to a sensual French rose called 'Gloire de Dijon.'

It's an ongoing love affair that persists today. In fact, look closely at certain roses—particularly the older, blousier, untamed kinds called climbers, cabbages, and ramblers—and you can't help thinking (a bit guiltily, perhaps) about sex.

At least, some of us can't. Over the years, the image of roses has been sadly sanitized by the horticultural industry (blame all those rows of regimented hybrid tea roses with cutesy names like 'Truly Yours' and 'Warm Wishes'). Gardening books, with their bland, stick-to-the-facts descriptions, are at fault too. Yet cen-turies ago, roses had a far more risqué presence in people's lives.

did THE GREEKS START IT ALL?

Aphrodite, the Greek goddess of love and beauty, is said to have initiated the belief that, for romance, it had to be roses. Red roses, especially. That's because one day, so the story goes, she pricked a toe on a rose thorn and her blood dripped onto the petals, staining them forever.

But in another equally thorny version of the tale, it is Aphrodite's son, Cupid, who claims the credit for instigating the rose-as-romantic-symbol idea—because of a bee. While Cupid was pushing his little button nose into a newly opened rose, this insect is believed to have stung him on the lip. So over-protective Momma Aphrodite rushed over to do what mothers the world over do—kiss it better—and in doing so, she removed the bee's stinger, turning it into a thorn on the rose's stem. Other bees buzzing about got similar treatment—and thus roses with thorns were born. An insufferably cute story, perhaps, but certainly a novel way to soften a painful introduction to the plant world.

Whatever the origins of the rose and its thorns, the first people to receive roses as gifts were male, not female. That was because the good old double standard was alive and well in ancient Greece: women, considered fit only for keeping house and bearing children, were cloistered firmly indoors by their

Weaving a garland long ago
somehow I found Eros
there among the roses.

I clutched him by his wings
and thrust him into wine
and drank him quickly.

And ever since, deep inside,
I feel the wings of Eros
gently tickling.

ANAKREON, CA. 570 BC,
"WEAVING A GARLAND
LONG AGO"

husbands, under lock and key, while men were free to do whatever they wanted. For affluent ones, that often meant keeping
young male lovers, upon whom they showered roses. Lots and
lots of luscious roses. In fact, if you were a pretty boy with a
good body, armfuls of the flowers got delivered to your door.
Admirers also gave you a chaplet (a garland designed for the
head) of fragrant rose petals to swan around in during rollicking male-only banquets. Girls, as ever, got the short end of the
stick. Women unfortunate enough to be born in ancient Greece
could earn a living making those chaplets yet kicking up their
own heels was definitely not in the cards.

PARTY GIRL CLEOPATRA *romped* ON A BED OF ROSES

When the Romans—always a libidinous lot—came along, they
strengthened the link of roses with sex. Once Venus assumed
the role of their Goddess of Love from Aphrodite, they dedicated the rose to her and, as Romans were wont to do, partied
every night, making sure there was an ample supply of their
new love symbol on hand, along with copious jugs of *vino*.
Roman men also wore rose chaplets, to overpower, it is said,
"the stink of stale wine in their hair."

Yet in a refreshing twist, these rose-tinged revels of the
Roman Empire differed from those of the Greeks because

women got to join in the fun and games too. The most famous party girl of them all was Cleopatra. There's a much-quoted story that she enticed Mark Antony into bed by spreading a two-foot-deep layer of rose petals over her bedchamber floor. And as if that wasn't inducement enough, she ordered her slaves to dip the sails of her celebrated barge in rosewater to perfume the sea breezes wafting through Rome harbour as Antony sailed away. This olfactory-themed wooing obviously did the trick. The love affair between Cleopatra and Mark Antony is one of the most celebrated in history, and nestling at the heart of this enduring tale of passion is the rose.

Other famous Romans got similarly hooked on this flower. Cleopatra's previous lover, Julius Caesar, wore rose chaplets to cover, it is claimed, his premature baldness. One governor of Sicily reportedly travelled around the countryside enthroned on a cushion stuffed with rose petals. He also kept "a fine-meshed bag of delicate linen gauze" containing more petals clasped to his nostrils. (Perhaps the latter was in self-defence, because the peasants he encountered didn't get to bathe very often.) And in a variation on the princess-and-the-pea fairy tale, this same arrogant gent fretted that he couldn't sleep because a lone petal in his rose-petal-stuffed mattress somehow got folded in half, causing a dent in his delicate bottom. It's a wonder that the long-suffering folks he lorded over didn't get themselves a sack of those petals too—and use them to smother the jerk.

Such was the all-pervasiveness of roses back then that it became the custom for an ordinary young swain out strolling with his girl to refer to her as "*mea rosa*." And as demand for roses kept on growing, increasingly large tracts of land around Rome were given over to their cultivation. The poet Horace grumbled that the fields of Italy were "being transformed into one vast nursery." City pooh-bahs worried, too, that roses encouraged drunkenness—because peasants would haul great panniers of cut blooms into market, sell them for big profits and then head home "well-soaked with wine, with staggering gait and pockets full of cash."

And the pooh bahs did have a point. The Roman obsession with roses wound up having lethal consequences. The famously decadent emperor Nero spent six million sesterces (the equivalent of hundreds of thousands of dollars) on roses for a single party, because he liked to drop their petals from the ceiling during his bawdy bashes. Literally millions of petals were required for these legendary orgies and guests of both sexes—dead drunk, doubtless having enjoyed a bit of *in flagrante delicto* on those celebrated Roman couches—actually suffocated under the weight of this fragrant onslaught. But it must have been a wonderful way to go. Lucius Apuleius, who wrote *Metamorphoses*, the only novel in Latin from that era that still survives today, described the scene thus: "Venus . . . heavy with wine and all her body bound about with flashing roses." Lewd, but lovers of the finer things of life. That sums up the Romans.

> The proper way to smell a rose is to take the bloom in the hand well up to the neck, bury the nose deep into its very heart and then smell gently, breathing in and out a bit harder than normally, just as you would sip a hot drink. It is not necessary to bruise the bloom, but do not be afraid to get the nose down into it.
>
> GEORGE W. FORREST

Proof of their rampant lust for roses remains to this day in the ruins of Pompeii, outside Naples. The real live roses that the town citizenry cultivated were incinerated when Vesuvius erupted, yet the volcano's dry heat preserved for eternity some remarkable rose paintings that had been artistically rendered, in colour, on the walls of Pompeii homes. Tourists can still view them—their colours faded for sure but still discernibly rosy—in the House of Venus Marina and the House of the Fruit Orchards. Also on show in another house at Pompeii (which for many years was out of bounds to female tourists) are graphic depictions of the carnal couplings that went hand in hand with roses during this deliciously decadent period of history.

a THORNY PROBLEM *for the* CHINESE

The attraction of roses for Romans was certainly sexual. Yet in China, they got mixed reviews. One besotted emperor reportedly called the rose "more beautiful than the smile of my favourite concubine," but regular Chinese folk were at one time suspicious of this plant that had the power to inspire such passion. What caused their wariness was not the voluptuous rose blooms themselves, but the thorns along the stems. That was because ordinary citizens regarded their enclosed courtyard gardens as the focal point of family life—and they believed that inviting a shrub covered in thorns into this orderly enclosure would inevitably create dissension within the family's ranks. Yet this reticence seems to have vanished quickly. Roses became as desirable to the Chinese as to everyone else. In fact, they are now thought to have originated in Asia. As early as BC 500, Confucius lauded the roses growing in the Imperial Gardens, and one of the oldest species in existence, *Rosa gallica*, still survives in the wild in some parts of China.

Throughout history, the sensual image of the flowers has persisted. In one Muslim legend, roses are said to have sprung from the sweat of Mohammed's brow. The Brahmin idea of paradise centres on a silver rose. A Hindu god, Vishnu the Protector,

Love Potion Number 4

Write best wishes to the couple in rose petals on the bed.
Make a roadway of more petals from the bed to the door.
On the flanges of the ceiling fan, place still more petals,
so they fall on the couple when they turn the fan on.

WEDDING DECORATION INSTRUCTIONS ON HINDU WEB SITE

apparently thought so highly of roses, he created his bride Lakshmi
from precisely 108 large rose petals and 1,008 small ones—a
charming belief that's as colourful as the idea of Eve emanating
from Adam's rib. In Peru, Eve has been depicted in the Garden of
Eden holding not an apple but a rose. And if you speak Urdu, the
word *gul* is still used to denote both a rose and a beautiful girl.

the ROSE SHEDS *its* RACY IMAGE

This happened when the killjoy Christians came along, after the
Romans. Although they were clearly captivated by the beauty of the
rose, church fathers decided it was time to put a lid on the lascivi-
ous nonsense and opt for much sterner stuff. Thus this hitherto
sexually charged flower, companion of bouts in the boudoir for
both the Greeks and Romans, metamorphosed into one of the

symbols of the Virgin Mary. Purity and chastity. That's what the rose was all about to the early Christians, and for hundreds of years, they included it alongside her in everything from medieval masterpieces to religious works by celebrated Renaissance painters.

However the rose's association with romance clearly lived on. Even during the dour Middle Ages, when people slunk around in sackcloth and ashes and got whipped for not reading the Bible at breakfast, woodcuts portrayed chaste-looking chaps collecting roses and offering them to demure maidens. And in a rare German illuminated manuscript, which survives from 1420, two monks are actually shown kissing what appear to be nuns, surrounded by arbours of—what else?—lush pink roses.

Another rosy relic that has survived that downtrodden era is the highly suggestive *Roman de la Rose*. Heavy on metaphor, this interminably long love poem popped up in France during the thirteenth century and tells the tale of a man who endures many trials and tribulations before finally consummating his passion for a loved one—who is symbolized by a rose.

Let's hope the poor overwrought gentleman enjoyed the experience.

Old roses are rich as a fig broken open, soft as a ripened peach, freckled as an apricot, coral as a pomegranate, bloomy as a bunch of grapes.

VITA SACKVILLE-WEST

the ROSE BOUNCES BACK

The Elizabethans—bless their hearts—restored the rose to its rightful place. Bad-boy poet and dramatist Christopher Marlowe paid tribute to its erotic qualities in a sonnet called *The Passionate Shepherd to His Love*, which included the promise:

> I will make thee beds of roses
> And a thousand fragrant posies . . .

And who can forget Shakespeare's evocative lines from *A Midsummer Night's Dream*?—that little stanza, recited by reluctant schoolkids everywhere, which is surely as romantic and memorable as any encounter with a real, garden-grown rose.

> I know a bank whereon the wild thyme blows,
> Where oxlips and the nodding violet grows;
> Quite over-canopied with luscious woodbine,
> With sweet musk-roses and with eglantine.

MEANWHILE, ACROSS *the* CHANNEL

The rose's reputation began to rebound in France too, particularly during the eighteenth century. And what precipitated this role reversal from a symbol of purity to an inspiration for *amour* was a clutch of busty vixens like Madame de Pompadour.

The celebrated mistress of Louis XV grew roses in her garden and loved them to distraction. Whenever someone painted her portrait, a bloom or two was almost always included somewhere in the picture. Later, her successor, Madame du Barry (libidinous old Louis sowed a lot of wild oats), went further: she flounced around the French court wearing ball gowns embellished with rose-shaped

> See how the roses burn!
> Bring wine to quench the fire!
> Alas! the flames come up with us,—
> We perish with desire.
>
> HAFIZ,
> "SEE HOW THE ROSES BURN!"

diamonds and had herself painted as the Goddess Flora, complete with a wreath of pink-hued roses in her hair and more rosy garlands winding through her hands. A treacly-looking rococo painting of the era by Fragonard called *The Lover Crowned* is said to have been inspired by the beauteous Madame du Barry—and the whole canvas is awash in pink and red roses.

Other French artists fell in a big way for the rose's rumpled blooms. One was Henri Fantin-Latour, who endowed the petals of white roses with so much sensuality, they seem to jump off the canvas. The Impressionist painter Renoir, meanwhile, made roses a regular feature in his portraits of women. In a famous work called *La Loge* (which depicts a Paris theatre scene) the connection is blatant: Renoir positions a prominent rose in the cleft between a woman's breasts and picks up the flower's warm red and pinks in her cheeks and lips. A sexy-looking rose with a delicious scent was named after him—a fitting tribute to this much-admired artist, who apparently thought that roses had "great physical allure."

Finally, who can forget the *femme fatale* from the Caribbean who was probably the most passionate advocate of roses ever— Empress Josephine. Born in Martinique, this beauty captured the heart of Napoleon and became hugely instrumental in developing some 250 new rose varieties at Malmaison, her home outside Paris, varieties that we still grow today. In fact, the rose renaissance that occurred in France can be laid squarely at the door of the determined Josephine and her earthy Corsica-born peasant of a husband (who, while on his way back to her bed after a military campaign, reportedly sent her the message "Don't wash"). The pair shared a lust for roses, which started after Napoleon dispatched home to her rose seeds that he had come across in Egypt. And even after he had moved on to younger, riper pickings than his older-by-six-years wife, she continued to collect more. Josephine took up gardening with rapturous zeal as she got older, no longer content to leave the choosing and cultivating of new rose specimens to her retinue of gardeners. Under her care, Malmaison became one of the first gardens in Europe to include a section devoted entirely to these flowers. And her acquisitions—hundreds of them—endure today as a symbol of the captivating—if not long-lasting—union of France's most famous power couple.

A ROSE *is* A ROSE *is* A ROSE

Gertrude Stein famously said the above words. But she was wrong. Consider the case of one classic—and popular—Alba rose that is now called 'Great Maiden's Blush.' To a modern gardener, it's a charming sort of name. It conjures up a picture of a shy Victorian miss in a bonnet, picking a basket of her namesake to take inside her thatched cottage. Yet this rose once had an altogether more risqué, almost X-rated image. That's because she was known during the eighteenth century as 'Cuisse de Nymphe Émue'—literally "Thigh of an Aroused Nymph"—a moniker dreamed up by an eminent botanist of the time called Georges Louis Marie Dumont du Courset.

In an etching from the era, the esteemed Parisian *docteur* (*naturellement*, he was French) looks sad, hung-over, and decidedly unattractive to the opposite sex. But perhaps his doleful demeanour was the consequence of too much champagne and shagging the night before. For he wrote in his journals that his much-admired rose had "the sensuous feel, fragrance and flesh tones of a virginal woman experiencing her first sexual encounter."

The Meaning of Roses

'CAROLINA ROSE': Love is dangerous

'CHARLES LE FIEVRÉE': Speak low if you speak love

'DOG ROSE': Pleasure and pain

'GLOIRE DE DIJON': Messenger of love

'CAMPION ROSE': Only deserve my love

REGULAR RED ROSE: I am faithful to you

DEEP RED ROSE: Bashful shame

'LA FRANCE': Meet me by moonlight

WHITE ROSE: I am worthy of you

YELLOW ROSE: I am jealous

'JAPANESE ROSE': Beauty is your only attraction

Whew. Alas, we have since kissed de Courset's hot *cuisse* goodbye. The name endured in plant catalogues for a couple of centuries, but then the uptight Victorians came along—and trust them to put a damper on things. They frowned on sexual openness, and so coy allusions became the order of the day. Although the petals of this luscious rose go from a peachy hue to deeper pinkish tones at their edges (in the manner described so evocatively by their champion), we now know it by that prim and proper moniker, 'Great Maiden's Blush.'

SOME *saucy* ROSES

Most rose varieties commemorate people, places, or significant events. Plant breeders tend to name them after their spouses and loved ones, colleagues, historical figures, celebrities they admire, wealthy individuals who put up funds for research, sites where they work, and, in the case of a very famous rose called 'Peace,' after the treaty ending the Second World War. Yet a few manage to wind up with more inspiring descriptions. A sampling:

'Allen's Fragrant Pillar': A cherry red hybrid tea rose, with a yellow centre.

'Belle Amour': Found in a convent in France. An Alba rambling rose that's salmon pink.

'Burning Love': A floribunda that's velvety crimson.

'Don Juan': A dark red tea rose that positively smoulders, but is prone to mildew.

'Heart's Desire': A hybrid tea with velvety petals that are deep crimson.

'Hebe's Lip': Creamy white, stained with deep rose at the centre.

'Leda': A damask rose, with crimson petals that are blush pink when fully open.

ANTICIPATION

THE TITAN ARUM
The cheeky plant that makes ladies swoon

Amorphophallus titanum. Now, there's a name that con-jures up images of a carnal kind. And it certainly fits. The first word means, literally—yikes—"shapeless, deformed, or collapsing penis." As for the second, think "titanic propor-tions"—because this incredible plant is very, very BIG.

Then there's the smell. "Godawful" is the only way to describe the overpowering stench of a titan arum (this popular name was coined by British celebrity naturalist David Attenborough, who felt uncomfortable referring to the plant as "Amorphophallus" on his BBC TV show). If you're ever around one of these horrors, have a box of tissues handy. And don't do what plant lovers always love to do—bend over and sniff deeply—because the fumes have been likened to a rotting corpse.

The titan arum produces the tallest, widest flower ever seen on the planet. It was discovered in Sumatra in 1878 by an Italian botanist called Odoardo Beccari, while he tramped through horribly humid jungles in search of interesting plant specimens. And Beccari sure found himself a whopper. Exactly how enormous is it? Well, a 6-foot-tall man, standing on tiptoe with arms stretched above his head, usually can't reach the top of its suggestive central spike, which is politely known, in gardening terminology, as the inflorescence or spadix.

The titan arum is one of Mother Nature's most macho manifestations, that's for sure. Yet it's deliciously creepy, too. Perhaps she got the wicked urge to create the titan arum as a joke on Hallowe'en night—because that impudent spike is what emits the foul smells. Wafting outwards in waves, they may seem repugnant to us, but have an effect like Chanel No. 5 on the kind of flies and beetles that love feasting on dead animals. These low-lifes crawl right inside the spike and get covered in pollen while pigging out. Then they head for one of the titan arum's compatriots to repeat the procedure—and in doing so, the grains of pollen rub off and fertilize this second plant.

Yet there's many a slip, as the old saying goes. The jiggery pokery that's required for this amorous action plan to work is no sure thing with a touchy titan arum. The flies may fail to deliver for a variety of reasons, or perhaps the air temperature isn't quite right. So the whole point—pollination—doesn't happen. In fact, this plant may look macho, but it's as flighty as Kathleen Battle back in the days when she kept throwing hissy fits at the Metropolitan Opera. Like her, a titan arum may steadfastly refuse to perform unless its perfectionist requirements are met—and this seldom happens, because most of these jungle-loving plants are now confined to botanical garden greenhouses in northern climates. Then there's the added challenge of the scarcity of mature specimens that are in a position to perform at all—because it takes at least eight painstaking years to raise a new titan arum from seed.

> The force that through
> the green fuse drives the flower
> Drives my green age . . .
>
> DYLAN THOMAS

So when this long-awaited miracle—an actual flower—does occur, excitement reverberates in horticultural circles around the world. The media flock in like moths, TV cameras at the ready, and thousands of plant lovers stand patiently in line to rubberneck at the stink bomb during its blooming period. The queues snaked all around a greenhouse at Kew Gardens, outside London, in 2009, when a titan arum deigned to bloom. And the wait was worth it, fans say. The centre spike shot up like a rocket, taking only two or three days to reach its full height,

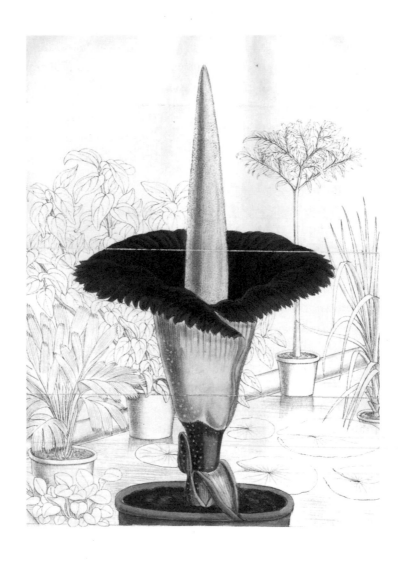

which is typical of titans. And while this energetic activity was going on, a sort of giant petal (in reality called a bract) surrounded the spike, looking rather like an upside-down pleated skirt, greenish-yellow on the outside, with a lining of deep purply red. This spike (or spadix) quickly thickened up, becoming fat and fleshy, and hundreds of little male and female flowers burst forth on the sides of its tube-like interior. Then came the nose-clogging fumes that are designed to draw those pollinating bugs in.

And that smell is powerful. Some people liken a titan's scent to "a mixture of rotten fish and burnt sugar." Others think decaying flesh. Take your pick. The gag-inducing scent usually doesn't last long, because a titan's performance is as fleeting as a fly in visit from a politician campaigning for re-election. The pushy spadix is all flash and bluster—its titillating tumescence lasting no more than two or three days. Then the whole thing abruptly withers and flops, all passion spent.

SNIFF *at your* PERIL

Consider the case of Matilda Smith, a well-known watercolour painter during the Victorian era who was commissioned by a leading publication of the day, *Curtis's Botanical Magazine,* to paint a titan arum.

Summoned to Kew Gardens in 1887, at the moment that a titan started to unfurl its dubious delights, the stoic—and undoubtedly corseted—Miss Smith sat down to sketch. Soon, though, the fumes got the better of her, and she fainted. But you have to hand it to those sturdy Victorian females. They were made of strong stuff. Like other women artists of that era, the intrepid lady persevered at her assignment, perhaps dabbing a lace hanky periodically to her nostrils. The results proved to be remarkable—watercolour portraits of the titan so accurately and beautifully rendered, they still have pride of place in Kew's archives today.

The plant that made her suffer survives, too. People ooh and aah over this particular titan arum in the Princess of Wales Conservatory at Kew. Yet, it's an ill-humoured grouch most of the time and rarely produces flowers.

What's no longer on show at Kew, though, is an impressive life-size drawing of the same plant. Measuring 18 feet long by 15 feet high, it depicted two brawny men hauling the titan's centre spike through the Sumatran jungles, lashed to a pole. Erected on the roof of Kew's Orangery—so overwhelming was public fascination with the latest botanical marvel to grace England's fair shores—the drawing could perhaps claim the distinction of being one of the first advertising billboards ever and certainly pulled in the crowds. It was also a novel form of promotion for a botanical garden to undertake. Yet Queen Victoria's prudish shadow loomed over everything—even horticultural happenings—during the latter part of the nineteenth century. The drawing of the titan was eventually deemed a bit too risqué to remain on the roof. Someone decreed that it had to be torn down. And, alas, it was.

GROWING a SKYSCRAPER ARUM

Don't try it unless you've got pockets as deep as Donald Trump and a ton of space. The titan arum demands its own private greenhouse (no one, even the nasally challenged, could stand the stink inside a home). Bear in mind, too, that, in botanical gardens around the world, the keepers of these tropical tantrum-throwers go through incredible conniptions attempting to keep their charges healthy and happy. And despite this devotion, the titan arum refuses to play nice most of the time and reward their reverence with a performance.

However, if you're drawn to the idea of a stinky weirdo to show off to the neighbours—and we gardeners do love going the "extra mile" for something different—an *Amorphophallus konjac* will do the trick. It's a smaller version of titan arum—but identically equipped. Same lewd, fleshy spike (reaching about 4 feet tall), same skirt-like surroundings, same disgusting stink, same shock value. The spike, according to garden writer Ken Druse (who's the proud owner of an *A. konjac*), looks like "a green and silver spotted baseball bat." The whole plant could be described as a knock-out, in fact, and a great way to impress the people gardeners always like to impress—other gardeners.

then THERE'S JACK . . .

Jack-in-the-pulpit *Arisaema*: a diminutive, distant relative of both *A. titanum* and *A. konjac*. Not limited to tropical green-houses, though, and joyfully jubilant about flowering out of doors in northern climates. Another plus for city gardeners is that Jack produces his strange "blooms" even under big trees. Once again, you get a some-what salacious spike popping up—only this time, the whole kit and caboodle manages to look vaguely sinister too, because the spike is partly concealed under a mysterious hood that flops toward the front of the plant.

Some people say this covering gives the *Arisaema* the appearance of a cobra rearing up. (One of its nicknames is cobra lily.) Others liken the upright stance of the spadix and its encir-cling "skirt" to a preacher standing in a church pulpit. In one beautiful Japanese variety, *A. sikonianum*, the spike is pure white, with a rather naughty-looking knob on its end. But in the olfactory department, jumpin' Jack won't knock your socks off because his scent is barely noticeable.

He does, however, harbour a firm reputation as an aid to love. The common name for this plant in Britain is cuckoo pintle (or pint)—and pintle is a colloquialism for penis. It was also once known as willy lilly, wake robin (the seventeenth-century play *Love's Metamorphosis* includes the line "They have eaten so much wake robin, they cannot sleep for love"), and the brutally blunt dog's dick. With much giggling, girls in rural England warned each other against touching "dick" (and even avoided looking at the plant when it grew in their schoolyards) because if they took a peek, the belief went, they'd wind up with a bun in the oven.

Love Potion Number 5

For men only: Enlist the aid of willy lilly in winning your lady. That is, remove the centre spike from a plant that's in flower and place it in the bottom of your shoe before an encounter with her. She will then be irresistibly drawn to you.

OLD COUNTRY BELIEF

more SWOONING—THIS TIME *by* A QUEEN

Poor Queen Isabella of Spain. Back in 1590, she's said to have passed out cold like Matilda Smith when presented with a plant. But what triggered her attack of the vapours was not the plant's overpowering smell. It was the sight of a weird, leafless object covered in prickles that apparently took the diminutive queen's breath away. The plant was a cactus—the first one introduced into Europe, brought back from the New World by Christopher Columbus. And while history is a bit hazy about the kind of cactus Columbus gave her, the culprit is thought to have been a small, ordinary-looking *Melocactus* or *Opuntia*, which grew in the West Indies.

But hold on a minute. What if, instead, Columbus hefted a humongous columnar cactus into the Spanish court? There's a distinct possibility that he could have. After all, these plants grew by the thousands in arid areas of Mexico, where the explorer and his cronies were busily plundering gold and bossing the Indians around. And the conquistadors owned, of course, those great big galleons to bring their booty back home. So what if the queen had an encounter with one of those amazing cacti? In that case, her celebrated fainting fit seems quite understandable. Perhaps she just wanted to giggle. Or was gripped by a mad urge to laugh out loud. But, being her imperial majesty, she couldn't do either. So Isabella took the easy way out and swooned flat on to the cold hard mosaic tiles of her palace floor, because she was so knocked out by the appearance of this plant. Fat, bulging, often with an end curving suggestively upwards, and laughably, unbelievably LARGE, columnar cacti do tend to come across, to most people who view them, as caricatures of—ahem—monster male appendages. Nowadays, their concupiscence strikes us as comical. We titter openly. Yet stiff fifteenth-century court protocol undoubtedly made acknowledgement of such allusions taboo, and certainly not the sort of thing a monarch did in public. *Madre mía*, no. In fact, this presentation from Columbus—if it happened—must have shocked the Spanish queen right down to the tips of her dainty black velvet slippers.

Was Isabella's reputedly ardent admirer trying to send her a subliminal message with his unique gift? Heart full of excited anticipation, did he hope she'd fall into his arms with desire? Probably not. But it's fun to speculate.

SEXY SPECIMENS, *but* NOT TO THE EXPERTS

Prissy as Victorian clergymen, modern garden writers seem as uptight as the Queen of Spain about the hit-you-in-the-eye cheekiness of columnar cacti. All cacti, in fact. Many kinds, not just the desert-dwelling whoppers, develop suggestive-looking protuberances at various stages in their growth. These often thrust themselves out of the base of the plant or its sides. Then they flop, fat and provocative, over the sides of flowerpots. Yet it's a characteristic that is completely ignored—and seldom depicted—in gardening books. The only hint comes in a few guarded words. Try "vigorous" and "impressive" for starters. Occasionally, if the writer is being very daring, "swollen" gets thrown in. But that's about it in the adjective department.

Love Potion Number 6

Saguaro cactus blossoms symbolize hope for a better tomorrow, a pledge of togetherness, and a promise to endure through the prickly thick and thins of life. Give your love a little bunch of these flowers on Valentine's Day.

INSTRUCTION ON A FLORIST'S WEB SITE

Baffling? Certainly, given the multiplicity of these monsters growing in the southern United States and Mexico. In fact, the only people willing to acknowledge their overt sexuality are, it seems, photographers, artists, and ordinary spectators who post pictures on the Web, often with cringe-making captions like "Viagra champ." Perhaps it's a case of the cactus experts—who are mostly men—shying away from stating the obvious out of sensitivity or embarrassment. (And admittedly, fellas, all those prickles are enough to make anyone squeamish.)

The Aztecs were less coy. Their Codex Magliabecchi, which dates from just after the Spanish conquest, contains several salacious references to cacti. They worshipped certain species and, during fertility ceremonies, they would cut up and eat the plants or smoke the dried flesh. One cactus in particular, the *Lophophora williamsii*, commonly known as peyote (which is small, smooth, rounded on top like an orange and not in the least bit lascivious-looking), is still used as a hallucinogen by the Huichol Indians of Mexico. Hippie types enraptured by the ponderous prose of Carlos Castaneda are also partial to getting high on it—and no doubt having a rollicking good time in the process.

why CACTI GROW *the* WAY THEY DO

It's a matter of survival, pure and simple. Columnar cacti are the camels of the plant kingdom. Many live in desert regions that receive only a sprinkle of rain a year—and sometimes not even that. The bulbous shapes that make us chuckle function like gigantic water tanks, storing moisture for months, even years, at a stretch.

Everything about a cactus is, in fact, created with water conservation in mind. It has no leaves because those need rain to grow. Their fearsome-looking prickles provide shade from unrelenting sun and heat. (So do the Santa Claus beards that develop on some species.) And the skin of a cactus is coated with a kind of wax, to prevent moisture evaporating from the surface.

PRIAPIC PROTUBERANCES *of* THE PRICKLY KIND

Dotting the landscape in the desert regions of the American Southwest, Mexico, and farther south, these cacti are a wonderful sight—and some are now protected by law to ensure their survival.

Carnegia gigantea: Photogenic cactus, popularly called saguaro, shaped like a candelabra. Mainstay of cowboy movies and

Mexican restaurants. Can take more than a century to reach its full grandeur of 40 feet or so.

Cereus validus: Tall (up to 25 feet), tubular, with huge, terrifying black spines spaced at even intervals down each column. Predominantly pink, tubular flower buds are the most erotic part, sprouting upwards from the column sides.

Cleistocactus: Covered in fuzzy spines, these grow in clumps. Their come-hither shapes look alert, jaunty, and ready to get down to business.

Espostoa: A blush-making beauty, strongly phallic. Nicknamed snowball cactus (or old man Peruvian cactus), its wide columns can soar over 25 feet skywards and bulge in a provocative way at the endo.

Mammillaria matudae: Snakes along the ground or over rocks. Rounded, 7-foot-long tubes that look positively lecherous. Then there's the sauciness of its name (which means "breasts" in Latin) and its very feminine pink flowers.

Pilosocereus: Amply endowed, bluish. Prickly, fattened at the tips, and covered in a "beard." Funnel-shaped pink and white flowers, which usually smell disgusting.

MORE *sexy* SHOCKERS

Arum lily *Alocasia*: Another impudent aroid, related to the titan arum. Popular nowadays as an exotic addition to decks in summertime, it produces leaves that are huge, handsome, dark green, and shiny as patent leather. Yet if the plant is allowed to grow large enough, it will also produce a waxy, white, trumpet-shaped centre spike. This protuberance is wide at the top, then narrows in the middle before bulging provocatively at the bottom, where its female parts are hidden. And though these organs are tucked away out of sight, the phallic spike was considered so prurient by the Victorians that refined ladies were advised to cut the offensive protrusions off before using *Alocasia* leaves in floral arrangements. After all, it wouldn't do to have the plants in the parlour disrupting tea and crumpets with the vicar.

Shameless penis *Phallus impudicus*: The name says it all with this one too. It's not a plant, though, but a large mushroom. And its licentious behaviour is awe-inspiring (and hilarious) to behold if you happen to stumble across a patch of *P. impudicus* while taking a walk through the woods in late summer.

The mushrooms usually burst on to the scene in September in North America (one of their favourite places to lurk is a layer of dead and rotting leaves). They resemble eggs when first emerging from the ground. But then comes the pornographic part: the thickness, proportions, and stance of *P. impudicus* do indeed bear such a striking resemblance to the human male organ, it's impossible to keep a straight face around them. Yet, as with the titan arum, what's equally arresting is their horrible smell. This emanates from a knob at the end of the shaft, which is coated in a yucky, dark green jelly that feels slimy if you're brave enough to touch it. The revolting substance is there—predictably—to lure the kind of flies that dine on rotting dung. After having their fill, they fly off and excrete the mushroom spores, undigested and intact, somewhere else. The result is more cheeky patches of *P. impudicus* to make hikers double up with laughter when they're out taking the air the following September.

Yet *carpe diem* if you want to see this phallic phenomenon. All erections are prone to droop dramatically after the job is done, and this one is no exception. Visit a *P. impudicus* the day after all the strutting and feasting has been going on, and it looks shrivelled and worn out. But the whole episode was undoubtedly a whole lot of fun—for the flies, that is—while it lasted.

Love Potion Number 7

Dry the flesh of a *P. impudicus* mushroom in the open air,
or use a smoker. Reduce this to a powder and take in a
glass of spirits. It will act as an aphrodisiac. OLD BELIEF

Tree of Heaven *Ailanthus altissima*: Unrelated to aroids, this
tree rivals the titan arum in the nostril-assaulting stakes.
Indeed, there is nothing very heavenly about the pungent
pong of this tree's branches, which have musky overtones
when adorned with flowers, usually in June or July. Most
people who walk underneath an *Ailanthus*—and a lot do,
because the tree is a favourite with city parks departments
across North America—gripe that the smell is exactly like
semen (although "rotting peanuts" also gets its share of
votes). So much so, on the West Coast, where *Ailanthus*
grows everywhere, it has earned the nickname "The Sperm
Tree of Los Angeles."

However, the *Ailanthus* isn't universally despised. A New
York writer, Betty Smith, lionized one towering specimen in
her 1943 best-seller *A Tree Grows in Brooklyn*. And in China,
where these trees originally come from, they are valued for
medicinal purposes and as habitats for silk worms.

DECEPTION

THE VENUS FLYTRAP
The femme fatale *who eats live prey*

Tipitiwichet. An odd word. Useful to remember for a Scrabble game, perhaps, when you're stuck with an excess of the letter *i*. Yet if swear words are banned from the game, forget impressing other players with *tipitiwichet*, because this tongue-twisting combination of letters is actually an obscenity. In Elizabethan times, it denoted, in a derogatory way, a certain part of female anatomy—and wasn't the kind of word used in polite company.

Unless, that is, you were talking—probably in an excited whisper—about a plant. A peculiar plant that's both as erotic and creepy as an Anne Rice novel. *Tipitiwichet* was the nickname given to the Venus flytrap. It all started in 1768, during the reign of Queen Elizabeth I, after her botanist, William Young, took home to Merrie England a few specimens of this North American botanical novelty that he'd discovered growing in the wilds of the Carolinas. People loved the plant's prurient appearance and, of course, its astonishing *modus operandi*.

That's hardly surprising. Just take a close look at a Venus flytrap. It produces pairs of flattish disks, resembling half circles, with wicked-looking barbed spikes ranged along their outside edges. These disks often look pink, fleshy, and decidedly seductive on their inward-facing sides. They somewhat resemble a woman's vulva, stippled with fine hairs—so the slang name that the bawdy Elizabethans dreamed up doesn't seem short of the mark. All things considered, the Venus flytrap is one sexy specimen, a characteristic that's borne out by her common name. Venus was, after all, the lusty Roman goddess of love. Then there's her Latin moniker, *Dionaea muscipula,* inspired by Dione, who happened to be the mother of Venus. (The latter part of the name means "mousetrap.")

I love flowers for their treachery
their fragile bodies
grace my imagination's avenues

ETEL ADNAN,
"THE SPRING FLOWERS OWN"

Imbued with eroticism, yes. Yet this floral *femme fatale* stands for an unsavoury side of sex, too, because she's a sadist.

A deceiving dominatrix no less. And a brutal murderer to boot. Because what the Venus flytrap does is entice living, breathing victims with her sweet juices, which are exuded on that "vulva," and once they land there and get themselves stuck in this gluey stuff, she closes those powerful jaws and crushes them to death. Slowly. Agonizingly. Then she smacks her chops and tucks into them for dinner.

Not a very nice lady. And this botanical booby trap has plenty of company. All carnivorous plants (as they are collectively known) operate in a similar fashion, and they're as ruthless and single-minded as a lion pursuing a gazelle on the Serengeti Plain. This is highly unusual behaviour for plants to adopt. Like Hannibal Lecter, the human monster in *The Silence of the Lambs*, the carnivorous ones are freaks of nature and certainly the strangest members of the plant kingdom.

Why do they do it? Why, unlike other plants, have they evolved to use insects and animal species as "food" in this gruesome way? Botanists, entomologists, and horticulturists have been trying to figure out the reasons for centuries. The plants puzzled Linnaeus, Darwin, and a feisty female scientist called Mary Treat, who lived in New York during Victorian times and conducted ghoulish experiments feeding scraps of meat to one species, the *Pinguicula*. And thanks to their thoroughly creepy appearance and habits, which have the ability to both repel and fascinate (usually at the same time), they have inevitably found their way into popular culture, playing starring roles in everything from *The Day of the Triffids* to *The Little Shop of Horrors*.

INNOCENT-SOUNDING NAMES, *but* CRUEL TACTICS

There are more than 630 species of carnivorous plants in the world—a staggering number. Although most people rarely get to see any of them, these plants are found everywhere from North American bogs to tropical Madagascar. And what a confusing bunch, concealing their killer instincts behind a slew of innocent-sounding common names like sundews, pitcher plants, rainbow plants, bladderworts, liverworts, and the rather charming water-wheel plant. Most grow in the wild and are quite small and easy to miss, especially if they're in long grass. Some exude a sort of sexiness like the Venus flytrap. Pitcher plants, for instance, seduce their victims with tubular appendages that resemble used con-doms. The poor bastards teeter on the edge of these wrinkly receptacles, then topple over and drown at the bottom in a smelly liquid. Yuck. Yet most carnivorous plants look just plain weird and the entrapment techniques they use are equally bizarre. Just ask someone who studies these plants for a living and she'll rattle off a formidable list: pitfall traps, flypaper traps, snap traps, bladder traps, lobster traps, suction traps . . .

What gets snared in these deadly devices? A cornucopia of candidates. While it's commonly assumed that carnivorous plants consume nothing more than annoying flies and other undesirable insects, the truth is less palatable. For example, one of the favourite foods of a Venus flytrap growing in the wild is butterflies. Watching these frail, fluttering creatures land unwittingly on her trigger hairs and then get crushed between her jaws like an old car in a scrapyard is not a pretty sight. Other species are known to enjoy munching on bees, wasps, earwigs, crickets, praying mantises, lizards, mice, crustaceans, many kinds of beetles, and even large rats. Anything, in short, that can fit into their cunning traps is fair game. Better lock up the cat.

devious DAMSELS *to* WATCH OUT FOR

A sampling of carnivorous plants and the devices they use:

The Glue Girls: These are small plants like sundews (*Drosera*) and butterworts (*Pinguicula*). They depend on adhesive traps, which are positioned on the ends of little glandular knobs sticking up from the plant's leaf surfaces. The glue glistens like dewdrops on the knobs, enticing the gullible.
The Pitcher Posse: Often painted by artists because they look so peculiar, pitcher plants are the ones that develop long,

condom-like tubes, or rounded pouches reminiscent of drooping testicles, covered in a network of little veins. The most common kinds are the *Sarracenia* and *Nepenthe* species. The rims of these hanging contraptions are slathered with nectar to lure prey.

The Snappy Seducers: The venerated Venus flytrap (*Dionaea muscipula*) and the waterwheel plant (*Aldrovanda vesiculosa*) are both specialists in lickety-split reactions when a prospective meal blunders in. They're equipped with spring-like traps that can shut in a flash, if necessary, and then the plants secrete juices to digest their victims.

The Vacuum Cleaners: Suction traps are the preferred method of bladderworts (*Utricularia*). These bladder-like apparatuses are more forceful than a Dyson, whooshing their victims inside the plant in a fraction of a second. Then a door shuts behind them, sealing their grim fate.

no BIG MACS, THANK YOU

Growing your own venal Venus is possible—perhaps. Of all the carnivorous plants on the planet, they are probably the easiest to cultivate and thus prized as houseplants. But squeamish folks should forget the whole idea, because owners do have to play chef when they get the munchies. That is, supply a steady diet of flies. Dead or alive, it doesn't matter much, but the average Venus flytrap needs to chomp through three or four of these tidbits a month to stay in trim.

Don't be tempted, though, to ply her with morsels of hamburger or any other kind of meat, as Mary Treat did. Experts say this plays havoc with the flytrap's delicate innards—and will probably kill the plant.

more DECEIVERS *of the* BOTANICAL KIND

Cruel plant *Araujia sericifera*: Native to Brazil and Argentina, this is a pretty and sweet-smelling plant, with white or pale pink blossoms. Yet it's deadly for night-flying moths who glue themselves to the flowers' sticky pollen while poking around trying to reach nectar. When the morning sun comes up, the pollen dries rock hard and the moths die—after a nasty struggle.

Devil's trumpet *Datura*: A member of the contradictory *Solanaceae* tribe, whose members can be benign (like tomatoes) or cause tummy troubles (like deadly nightshade), *Datura* stands out because it's a hallucinogen that can deceive people into

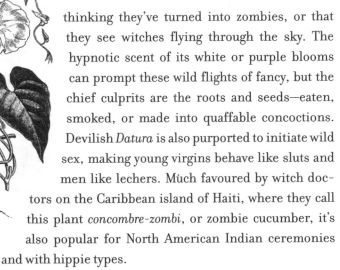

thinking they've turned into zombies, or that they see witches flying through the sky. The hypnotic scent of its white or purple blooms can prompt these wild flights of fancy, but the chief culprits are the roots and seeds—eaten, smoked, or made into quaffable concoctions. Devilish *Datura* is also purported to initiate wild sex, making young virgins behave like sluts and men like lechers. Much favoured by witch doctors on the Caribbean island of Haiti, where they call this plant *concombre-zombi*, or zombie cucumber, it's also popular for North American Indian ceremonies and with hippie types.

Another *Solanaceae* sister, *Brugmansia*, commonly known as angel's trumpet, is said to have similar, but milder, hallucinogenic effects on humans. True or not, this plant wins in the bigger, better blooms department. Shaped like trumpets, in white or pale orange, these beauties hang downwards from the plant's stems, looking like giant Christmas tree ornaments. And of the two, *Brugmansia* is far easier to grow as a tropical novelty on a deck in summertime than slow-to-germinate *Datura*. Cats love sprawling beneath the trumpets on a hot night, clearly enjoying the heady scent and (perhaps) getting gloriously stoned.

Fetter bush *Leucothoe*: A beautiful, fragrant shrub, but, alas, prone to tantrums that exasperate many gardeners. Perhaps her irritability stems from her ancient Greek origins. Libidinous *Leucothoe* is named after a flighty Persian princess who deceived her husband and took a lover. Outraged, he chased her off a cliff and into the surging ocean below. Apollo then came along, was charmed, and changed her into a sea goddess. But she behaved badly with him too. To get even, Apollo turned the silly airhead into a plant.

Love Potion Number 8

Drop pansy juice into the eyes of someone sleeping, and she (or he) will be deceived into thinking she's fallen in love with the first living thing she sees upon waking.

OLD ENGLISH BELIEF. IN SHAKESPEARE'S
A MIDSUMMER NIGHT'S DREAM, OBERON
USES THIS POTION TO MAKE TITANIA,
QUEEN OF THE FAIRIES, FALL IN LOVE
WITH BOTTOM.

SEDUCTION

THE CEREUS
The night-bloomer with the sizzling scent

What makes middle-aged males willing to stay up all night, feverish with excitement, once (or maybe two or three times) a year?

Oh, it's not that tiresome little blue pill we're all sick of hearing about. Instead, it's a cactus called *Epiphyllum oxypetalum*, commonly known as the night-blooming cereus. This plant produces flowers that are described as "powerfully erotic" to many masculine noses. In fact, the olfactory allure of the cereus is legendary, lauded not only by the Spanish conquistadors but Puccini's Tosca as well, who promised hot sex to her lover Caravadossi at his villa when the "fragrant flower of the night blooms."

Modern fans include writer John Cheever. In his *Journals*, Cheever mentions walking over to his neighbours' house, in suburban Ossining, New York, to witness the flowering of their cereus—an event that he wouldn't for the world miss. Presumably, getting a whiff of her powerful perfume was all part of the excitement. And Cheever's experience is pretty typical. Just about every male who has a fling with this plant tends to fall a little in love with her. It's partly due to that fragrance, because an encounter with a cereus is of necessity short-lived—truly a one-night stand of passion—since that's all she's prepared to grant to her admirers. In fact, the cereus is more sparing with her favours than possibly any other flower—and this mesmerizing event always takes place after dark. Flowers can be few and far between. Often you get only one. Then, following a few short hours of flaunting her charms—and that tantalizing scent—the flower withers away and dies as the sun comes up.

The night-blooming cereus is the stuff of steamy tropical nights, all right. Think Ava Gardner and Richard Burton coupling on that Puerto Vallarta beach in *Night of the Iguana*. And down Mexico way, they know this plant by the enchanting name *Reina de la Noche* (Queen of the Night) and, like Cheever's neighbours, hold parties when she blooms. A smart idea, for sure, because her performance is so unforgettable, it should be shared with someone—preferably a lover.

the EXCITEMENT *of* OPENING NIGHT . . .

But first, let's begin at the beginning: for most of her life, the cereus is no bodacious babe in the looks or fragrance department. For months on end, this plant (like a lot of cacti) will simply sit, utterly charmless and apparently sulking in a pot or outside in the garden, if you're fortunate enough to live in the tropics, producing uninspiring bits and pieces of stick-like growth stippled with short prickles. These sticks grow in segments and can look rather like a Christmas cactus on a bad hair day.

In truth, the cereus is the sort of houseplant about which frustrated owners wind up saying, "I'm fed up with that damn thing, Martha. Shall we get rid of it?" And Martha nods her head eagerly because she's secretly hated the silly cereus for years, it looks so ugly hanging in their conservatory, and now it's starting to crowd out her clivias. (Cereus are bossy plants. In the south, they can grow enormous, their messy limbs sprawling everywhere, and if planted in a container, watch out. You can break your back, hauling them around.)

But wait. Don't consign her to the compost heap, because one day this flighty space-hogger will start developing a bud.

And the tightly wrapped appendage, poking out from one of the stems, can grow almost obscenely large, swelling balloon-like to the size of an orange, over several weeks as the plant prepares to bloom. Fans get into the habit of inspecting these odd-looking protuberances every few hours, so eager—and anxious—are they about the spectacle ahead. It's fun, but they also have good reason to worry. Go away for the weekend, and you might miss the whole show. It usually happens like this: one evening, the bud decides to swell no more and looks ready to burst open. That's when John Cheever undoubtedly received his summons from the neighbours to "get over here right away." They knew he wanted to observe the magical event that was about to unfold. Because pure magic it is.

> The garden is so ferociously sexy at night, it's almost lurid.
>
> ANNE RAVER

TAKING *her* SWEET TIME *to* SEDUCE

When a cereus flower opens, this Plain Jane of a plant transforms herself into a wanton woman on a par with those silky *femmes fatales* of old Hollywood movies. As admirers look on, bleary-eyed, cameras at the ready, having waited up half the night (how she loves to keep us in suspense), the cereus unfurls her treasure—often just one solitary flower. She performs this act slowly, the petals tending to pop open one by one with rather jerky movements, hardly the seamless slithering of a burlesque dancer getting down to the bare essentials, but incredibly exciting to watch anyway. And they are creamy white, these petals, forming a huge cup that can measure as much as nine inches across.

The petals have a captivating sheen that some say look like silk. Yet according to North Carolina horticulturist Peter Loewen, the texture and appearance of a cereus flower are "like a baked meringue that's been brushed with egg white"—not exactly a titillating image, unless you're an ardent cook, but one that does happen to fit the cereus flower quite well.

Then come the stamens—hundreds of gossamer-thin threads packed tightly inside each bloom, all topped by little blobs of golden pollen. These spread out, in the space of an hour or two, to surround a long, thin, elegant pistil at the centre of the flower—and the sight of this shining mass reaching out into the night air (for practical reasons. this plant is eager to attract bats that will pollinate it) can be as breathtaking as the bloom itself.

And about that all-too-brief flower: it rarely lasts longer than twenty-four hours. Even so, its seductive aura can linger on. Gary Paul Nabhan, writing in *Journal of the Southwest*, got a thrill after stumbling across a cereus that had just bloomed in

Love Potion Number 9

For increased sexual energy, chew half a gram of fresh plant material from a cereus cactus. Or crush the same amount in a small amount of brandy and drink slowly. This stimulates the heart. OLD JAMAICAN RECIPE

an alleyway of Baja Arizona. It was "luminously pale and, at this hour, sort of ragged, like an old nightgown that has endured far too many midnight frolics," he wrote. "And yet it remains so sensuous—I dare say, erotic. A whole lot of negligee designers working for Victoria's Secret could never surpass its skimpy elegance."

Which sort of sums up the appeal of the cereus. Symbolizing "transient beauty" in the language of flowers, this extraordinary plant even has the ability to captivate its biggest admirers— men—when its short burst of glory is over.

SORTING OUT *the* CEREUS SPECIES

It's tricky. The truth is, the plants that we call "night-blooming cereus" can be more bewildering than a computer program that comes without a manual. A mind-boggling number of species

belong to the huge tribe of plants collectively known as *Cereeae*—
and not all of them come out to play after the sun goes down.

A few facts: cereus grow in different parts of the world
(although usually warmer climates). They have different char-

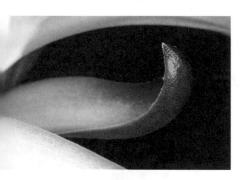

acteristics and growth habits (some
are sprawlers and produce small,
unremarkable flowers, others climb
trees and become prolific whoppers
with show-offy blooms, while a few
produce big, yummy red fruits). But
that's the easy part. Botanical names
in this far-flung family are intimi-
dating, to say the least. In fact, some
species sound more like prehistoric dinosaurs than plants: for
instance, *Selenicereus pteranthus* (in reality a snake-like cactus
with bronze flowers) and *Cereus pterogonus* (known as the tor-
toise cactus). Yet the kind that's most commonly used as a
houseplant is *Epiphyllum oxypetalum*.

LAST LOVE *of* A GUILLOTINED QUEEN

The word *cereus* comes from the Greek for "candle." The conquistadors, who stumbled across these plants growing in Mexican
jungles in the sixteenth century, probably gave the cacti that

name because they didn't simply get a charge out of their noc-turnal charms. The Spanish settlers cut and dried fleshy branches of many species of cereus, then dipped the ends in oil and used the tapers to light their homes.

Later on, as the fame of these plants spread, Queen Marie Antoinette fell madly in love with a cereus. She persuaded the great botanical artist Pierre-Joseph Redoute to do a painting of a specimen called *Selenicereus grandiflorus* while members of her court at Versailles looked on. Six weeks later, the Republic was proclaimed. The Queen lost her head. But the painting survived.

In the late nineteenth century, Miss Margaret Mee, an intrepid Victorian botanical artist, risked crocodiles, malaria, and the advances of untamed "savages" to travel up the River Amazon in search of a cereus. After several fruitless attempts, she finally found what she was looking for—a *Selenicereus wittii* with three buds about to flower. Fighting off armies of mosqui-toes, she nonchalantly unpacked her watercolours and easel, settled down in the swampy forest to sketch, and overnight produced another now-famous painting.

the CELEBRATED CEREUS HEDGE *of* HAWAII

Panini o kapunahou. Sounds like an Italian sandwich with a dubious filling. Yet this is the Hawaiian name for a species of cereus that forms what is certainly the world's longest, most fragrant, and most unusual hedge.

This botanical wonder straddles the top of stone walls surrounding Punahou College in Honolulu. It's a thick tangle of *Hylocereus undatus*—commonly known as red pitaya or dragon fruit (for its big edible fruits)—and stretches, amazingly, for over half a mile. When this gigantic hedge comes into bloom, usually over the course of several nights in July, crowds of rubberneckers flock to the college to stand around and ogle, because the sight and fragrance are, as one awed bystander puts it, "like being in a midsummer night's dream."

As many as five thousand huge white blooms will pop open on the hedge, often all at once, because these are very mature cereus that have thrived into a ripe old age. They were planted way back in 1838 by Mrs. Hiram Bingham, wife of a missionary assigned to Honolulu. During the reign of Queen Liluokalani, elaborate ceremonies were organized for the night the cereus flowered. The hedge is now lovingly maintained by the college and has become a tourist attraction.

During the Second World War, these cereus served another purpose: aromatherapy for bedridden servicemen. Students of the college picked the buds just before they opened and delivered them to local hospitals, where their exotic scent undoubtedly reminded the wounded soldiers of the wonderfully alive world waiting for them outside, once they got back on their feet again.

Indeed, the scent is a powerful draw. Hypnotic, heady, rather sweet, with a touch of spice, it will fill a room within minutes. Better yet, be standing in a tropical garden, under the moon and stars, when this fragrance kicks in. Take a deep breath and . . .

The fragrance of a cereus is what men who aren't in the habit of spouting pretty piffle about plants will admit to getting excited about. "It is downright erotic. The air gets filled with the most intoxicating perfume you could imagine, " exults Will Creed, a New York interior landscaper. Creed has lovingly nurtured several of these cacti in a lean-to rooftop greenhouse in Manhattan and says they're like no flower he has ever seen. But he adds, a little sadly, "By dawn, the flower is spent—I choose that word deliberately! And then the show is over."

Too bad. But as the old saying goes, the things in life that are worth having never last long. Like a precious cereus.

more SCENTED SIRENS

Once dusk descends, many mistresses of the moonlight are ready, willing, and able to lure us down the garden path with their exotic fragrances. A few choice ones:

Common lemon yellow or Citron daylily *Hemerocallis citrina*: Seen everywhere and a no-brainer to grow. Nothing special in the looks department, yet it emits a glorious sweet scent at night. Plant this in great big swaths and your whole garden will take on the atmosphere of the Arabian Nights.

Honeysuckle *Lonicera*: There are over 180 kinds of honeysuckle (now there's a name to inspire erotic thoughts). A clambering vine, it's the "woodbine" of Shakespeare's plays and in the language of flowers means "devoted love." Can get out of hand, though. Worth it for the scent, which is most powerful at night.

Common honeysuckle *Lonicera periclymenum*: Has familiar pink and yellow flowers and gallops up any structure. In William Faulkner's *The Sound and the Fury*, one character, Caddy, gets sexually aroused when she smells this plant. And in rural England, honeysuckle flowers used to be forbidden in homes where underage girls lived, because the scent caused the sweet young things to have erotic dreams.

Lady of the night *Brunfelsia*: A tropical shrub that can reach 8 feet high, her seductive perfume is only apparent after dusk (in the daytime she has no scent at all). Several kinds, white or purplish flowers. Grow as a potted plant in northern climates, but she will outgrow the container quickly.

Moonflower vine *Ipomea alba*: Related to morning glories. Pure white flowers, sweet scent. Several varieties, some with large, beautiful blooms. Buy started plants in spring, because it can be difficult to grow from seed.

Night jessamine or jasmine *Cestrum nocturnum*: Known as *sundel malam* (meaning "night whore") in Sudan because of her incredibly erotic scent at night. Small, unremarkable white flowers emit this fragrance in waves, and if you've smelled orange blossom, the impact is similar. However, some fans are more lavish in their praise, hailing what hits noses with an incredible wallop as "sweet musk mingled with heliotrope."

Hindus, meanwhile, call night jessamine "moonlight of the grove" and celebrate her in flowery verse. The plant also appears prominently in an erotic painting by Leonardo da Vinci of Leda, the goddess who fell in love with a swan. (She's shown, provocatively naked and looking as luscious as a ripe fruit, with both the bird and a flowering sprig in her arms.) Whatever her impact, however, Jezebel jessamine is definitely a damsel of the darkness. By day, her fragrance changes and becomes even unpleasant, and it's never as strong in the evening as during the witching hours. Easy to grow, this shrubby plant is capable of churning out flowers all year round but can be problematic confined to a container in northern climates, because she's no shrinking violet. Replant in a bigger pot if you don't get flowers.

And don't mix up night jessamine with regular jasmine. The botanical name of the daylight version is *Jasminum* (this plant is confusing, to say the least, because there are over two hundred species in this family), but the regular kind emits its scent during the day too.

Peacock orchid *Gladiolus callianthus*: Not really an orchid. Triangular white flowers with centres that are the rich, deep maroon of Victorian sofas. They look rather like a bunch of butterflies hovering at night, because you can't see the stems. Emits a gentle but enticing fragrance that's a perfect accompaniment to decadent dinner parties on the deck with lots of wine flowing, because the subtle scent won't overpower the *vino*. Originally from Ethiopia and subject to constant name changes by the plant pooh-bahs, its former name is *Acidanthera murielae*. Plant the little corms in a pot in spring. Easy to grow. Usually blooms in July or August.

Sweet or dame's rocket *Hesperis matronalis*: Such a stodgy, ridiculous Latin name, conjuring up images of corseted matrons waving Daughters of the Empire flags about. The common name fits better, but still doesn't seem particularly appropriate for this English cottage garden kind of plant. Very easy to grow (almost too easy for it self-seeds everywhere, if you aren't careful), rocket produces a jumble of lovely violet or pinkish flowers on messy, floppy stalks. Not for neatniks. Yet its scent is so powerful at night, garden visitors will invariably ask, "What's that lovely smell?"

Tuberose *Polianthes tuberosa*: It was said by the poet Shelley to be "the sweetest flower for scent that blows." Called the Mistress of the Night in Malaysia. Fell out of fashion for a while, due to its use at funerals, but now stems of the white, waxy, incredibly fragrant blooms are sold by many florists as cut flowers.

Wild tobacco *Nicotiana*: Smoking isn't a turn-on for anyone nowadays (unless you're Don Draper in the TV series *Mad Men*). Yet the perfumed flowers of wild tobacco plants are something else entirely, and certainly seductive. The best kind to grow is *N. sylvestris,* a towering annual. Can reach 7 feet tall. Looks like Miss Havisham in her washed-out wedding dress during the day, but come nighttime, her bunches of tubular white flowers perk up, pour out a bewitching jasmine-like scent, and transform her into the belle of the ball. Other shorter kinds of this plant have a similar fragrance, but avoid like the plague the nasty shortie hybrid versions of *Nicotiana* called Nikkis. Sold in garden centres everywhere, they have no discernible smell at all.

EROTIC, YES—BUT *not* REALLY AIMED AT US

Flowers that open and release alluring scents after sunset do so to attract pollinators like night-flying insects, bats, and moths. It's also why nocturnal flowers are usually white. (White flowers are more visible in the dark.) In fact, if you stand in a garden at night long enough to let your eyes become accustomed to the darkness, you might even spot a moth flying in to feed on a flower. Some moths are surprisingly large, with beautiful markings. For instance, hawkmoths *Agrius cingulatus* are common in North America and as big as hummingbirds. They also behave like hummingbirds—beating their grey or brown wings rapidly as they dart forward into a flower, then performing the miracle of flying backwards as they reverse out again and move on.

Come slowly—Eden!
Lips unused to Thee—
Bashful—sip thy Jessamines
As the fainting Bee—

Reaching late his flower,
Round her chamber hums—
Counts his nectars—
Enters—and is lost in Balms.

EMILY DICKINSON,
"COME SLOWLY—
EDEN (211)"

However, moths—like bats—tend to get a bad rap from humans. "Ooh, how creepy," we think and hurry indoors clutching our martinis if a big moth flaps into the garden near us. And admittedly, their sudden appearance can be a shock.

Nor do they look conventionally appealing, like their daytime cousins, butterflies, do. Yet these nocturnal visitors can be engrossing to watch. A night-flying moth is often equipped with an immensely long "tongue" known as its proboscis. It's built for probing deep into the centre of flowers, to get at the treasure trove of sweet nectar. Yet there's trickery at play in this procedure, for when the moth leans close and plunges its proboscis down into the flower, grains of pollen brush up against its body and legs. And the pollen sticks there. Firmly. So when the moth flies away to its next meal, the pollen hitches a ride and those tiny grains eventually get transferred to the pistil of another flower, thus setting fertilization in motion.

Yet it is the powerful scent that draws the moth to the flower in the first place. This olfactory lure devised by Mother Nature is irresistible to the winged creature of the night—and, coincidentally, can have the same effect on us.

the ODDLY NAMED TREE THAT'S TURNED INTO A FAMOUS FRAGRANCE

The people of the Philippines call it the *ylang ylang* (pronounced *ee-lang ee-lang*) and claim that its scent acts as a sure-fire incitement to love. Whether that's wishful thinking or not, one fact is indisputable: the flowers of this much-used tree are a key

ingredient in the production of what is probably the most popular perfume in the world—Chanel No. 5. Indeed, the legions of
ladies who for decades have dabbed the famous French fragrance behind their ears before
going out can thank the *ylang ylang*
if their dates become smitten.

Filipinos claim the *ylang
ylang* never fails to do the trick in
the dating department because
the flowers act as such a powerful aphrodisiac. In Samoa, where
the tree is known as *mosu-oe,*
couples once soaked the blooms
in warm coconut oil to absorb
their powerful perfume, then
rubbed this oil onto each other's
bodies before lovemaking. And
the painter Gauguin, who abandoned his middle-class family
in Paris and sailed off to the South Seas, was entranced when
nubile young Tahitian *vahines* observed this ritual before join-
ing him in bed.

A flower's fragrance declares to all
the world that it is fertile, available,
and desirable, its sex organs oozing
with nectar. Its smell reminds us in
vestigial ways of fertility, vigor,
life-force, all the optimism,
expectancy, and passionate bloom
of youth. We inhale its ardent
aroma and, no matter what our
ages, we feel young and nubile in a
world aflame with desire.

DIANE ACKERMAN,
A Natural History of the Senses

This is one prolific performer, too. A ten-year-old *ylang
ylang* tree is capable of churning out 23 pounds of its big,
greenish-yellow flowers in one year. However, this statistic

isn't as impressive as it may appear, because only about 2 per cent of the flowers' weight is oil. A perfume maker like Chanel, for instance, needs a staggering 200 pounds of oil to produce barely one pound of perfume essence for its trademark No. 5.

We can also dine on the bounty of the generous *ylang ylang*. A member of the huge (and often delicious) custard apple family, the tree goes by the botanical name of *Cananga odorata* and develops fleshy edible fruits, if its flowers aren't all snipped off to make perfume, that is. These get turned into fruit sorbets, drinks, and other concoctions throughout tropical Asian countries.

DESIRE

THE FIG
Did this fruit seduce Adam?

Cut open a ripe fig—and it's unmistakable. Even blatant. The moist pinkish purple flesh, with its enticing folds, looks rather like the private parts of a woman.

Indeed, when the innards of a fresh fig are staring you in the face, it's not hard to understand why Adam and Eve got up to that hanky-panky in the Garden of Eden. (The forbidden fruit couldn't possibly have been an apple, scholars now declare, since apples didn't grow in the area of the Middle East where the garden is believed to have been located.)

Adam's fall from grace perhaps went something like this: hitherto innocent and unaware, he stumbled across a fig tree.

Then after taking a bite of the luscious fruit and noticing its striking interior, he was immediately gripped by an extraordinary sensation. So much so, he had to grab a big green leaf from the tree to mask the tumescent tumult that was taking place in his nether regions.

But then Eve—naughty, naked Eve—sashayed out of his rib, took a bite of the fruit too, and—whoo hoo—we all know what happened next.

Thus, can mankind's first carnal caper be attributed, not to an apple—but to the dripping juiciness of a fig? Did the sight of same induce such an uncontrollable state of desire in Adam, he felt impelled to offer a bite to Eve, then drop his drawers (so to speak)—and change the course of the world?

Well, it's a thought. And true or not, figs can certainly lay claim to being among the most erotically charged fruits on the planet. Fresh figs (not those disgusting dried specimens, full of gritty seeds and sold in flattened brown slabs at health food stores) have been arousing mortals—particularly men—since time began.

Just pluck a ripe fig from a tree, preferably on a very hot, humid afternoon. Do it while lolling around on some flower-filled patio in the Mediterranean, Mexico, or Australia. Then, very slowly and deliberately, bring this delectable object to your mouth. Savour the utter deliciousness of the whole experience:

the skin's slight sheen; the soft, sensual feel of it in your hand; the unique taste—sweet yet not cloying—when you place the flesh between your teeth; the nectar that spills out in little dribbles as you bite down; and, finally, the luscious sensation of dozens of pearl-like seeds exploding in your mouth.

You'll soon get the picture.

ENTICING *to* MANY CULTURES

A fig's come-hither cleft. That's the biggest turn-on. It's visible in most figs after you slice them in half. And for thousands of years, in cultures all over the world, writers and philosophers have likened the appearance of this orifice, with its surrounding folds of flesh, to female intimate organs in a state of arousal. Although the entire fruit is associated with lust, fertility, and masculinity (whole figs hanging on a tree are said to resemble male genitals) what consistently grabs everyone's attention is that provocative crack, often barely noticeable, that opens across the middle. The Phoenicians' name for figs was *pagh*, which also meant "vulva." And in the Bible's lusty Song of Solomon, the author undoubtedly has this particular body part in mind when he says to his blushing bride. "The fig tree has ripened its figs. Arise, my darling, my beautiful one, and come with me."

Figs

The fig is a very secretive fruit.
As you see it standing growing, you
   feel at once it is symbolic:
And it seems male.
But when you come to know it better,
   you agree with the Romans,
    it is female.

The Italians vulgarly say, it stands for
the female part; the fig-fruit:
The fissure, the yoni,
The wonderful moist conductivity
towards the centre.

Involved,
Inturned,
The flowering all inward and
   womb-fibrilled;
And but one orifice. . . .

D.H. LAWRENCE

Even today, figs are linked explicitly with sex. There's an obscene gesture still employed in some parts of Italy, Spain, and the Middle East, in which hot-blooded males (particularly enraged car drivers after someone has cut them off) insult each other by balling up a fist and poking a thumb end between their first two fingers. It's a crude representation of female genitals, with the thumb playing the part of the clitoris. Italians call this gesture *fare la fica*—literally "do the fig." (In Latin, the word *fica* has a double meaning. It can denote either a fig or a woman.) But whatever the name, there is always a figgy connection.

The allure of figs clearly persists everywhere, even though most modern men rarely have the opportunity to pick this fruit from a tree. In his fascinating book *The Fruit Hunters*, young Canadian writer Adam Leith Gollner acknowledges the lusty feelings figs inspire when he visits an open-air market in Montreal and hears hawkers crying out that each piece of fruit contains "five grams of Viagra."

Then he meets up with a male friend who has just returned from Greece.

"Whenever I open a fig," confides the friend, "I want to f—it."

Memo to girlfriends: skip the stilettos. Buy your guy a basket of figs instead.

PITCHING *for* THE POMEGRANATE

Forget apples and figs. What really grew in the Garden of Eden, many academics now argue, was the pomegranate. And it's certainly possible that this odd fruit provoked Adam and Eve to get all hot and heavy with each other. After all, there's that suggestive reference in the Song of Solomon (4:13–14), "Your thighs shelter a paradise of pomegranates with rare spices"—which must rank as the most original come-on ever.

Yet Solomon has a good point. The pomegranate's treasure trove of little seeds, called arils, do indeed possess an erotic quality, especially if eaten slowly. Each aril is a juicy little jewel (likened to rubies in Muslim texts) that comes enmeshed in its own individual casing of bright crimson-purple flesh. Then the arils are jam-packed together in a round, leathery, reddish skin that's as tough as a baseball and looks rather like one. German poet Rainer Maria Rilke described this skin more eloquently as being like "Cordovan tapestries." However it strikes you, peeling the covering off and then sucking on the seeds is, sex gurus say, a perfect prelude to encounters of an amorous nature. As one Web site advises: "Pick pomegranate seeds out one by one, then feed them to your lover, while lying in bed."

Well, okay, but better watch the sheets. The juice of this

fruit stains—horribly. And spitting out those arils, once they're picked clean, is a smart idea too, because pomegranate seeds have a reputation as a fast-acting laxative.

But back to Adam. Modern medical knowledge about pomegranates does lend weight to the pomegranate-as-forbidden-fruit argument. In fact, had Adam known about them, he and Eve would doubtless have gorged themselves silly—and then been hard at it all night. That's because pomegranate juice is rich in antioxidants, which doctors say increase blood flow to the genitals. According to a California study of fifty-three men experiencing libido problems, over half of them got their mojo back after drinking several glasses of pomegranate juice a day. Small wonder the stuff is now sold in supermarkets for big bucks.

PROSERPINE *and* THE POMEGRANATE PIPS

Masochistic sex precipitated by pomegranates? Yes, perhaps. Consider the case of Proserpine. This Roman goddess with a name that sounds like air freshener (in Greek myths, she was known as Persephone) gets herself kidnapped by Pluto, grand pooh-bah of the underworld, who hauls her off to Hades and has his way with her. They marry. Then, although she wants desperately to escape and return home, poor Proserpine is held captive by Pluto for four months out of every year because, the

legend goes, he has persuaded her to eat six pomegranate pips.

The pips symbolize the underworld and the "dead" time of year—that is, winter, when there's nothing green growing—and, in this complicated myth, anyone who tastes the fruit of the underworld is doomed to remain there forever. Yet Proserpine manages to escape every spring thanks to her mother, Ceres, the goddess of fertility, who hammers out a deal with Pluto that allows her nubile daughter to return home for the growing seasons of the year. Thus Ceres's joy at the return of Proserpine in spring is the trigger for the world to turn green again, but once the summer's over and her beloved offspring has to head back to Pluto's clutches, she's filled with such despair that everything withers and dies.

The myth has been turned into a metaphor for both female captivity and the arrival of the growing season. Whatever the truth, luscious-lipped lady Proserpine looks both seductive and tragic in a famous 1877 painting by pre-Raphaelite Dante Gabriel Rossetti. Held provocatively in her hand is a pomegranate that's been cut open to reveal the seeds. Fleshy, red, and inviting yet somehow a little sinister, the seeds hint at dark dealings underground with her possessive paramour, Pluto.

Moral of the tale: spit out the pomegranate pips if your lover's a control freak.

QUIBBLING *over* QUINCE

Dry, hard, and mouth-puckeringly sour when raw. That's quince. But during cooking, this odd fruit (which looks like an apple or pear gone wrong) turns a romantic rosy red. Perhaps the transformation explains why quince has become yet another serious contender in the Garden of Eden forbidden-fruit stakes.

Could Adam and Eve have succumbed to a quince instead of the fabled apple? Some academics say yes because quinces were once regarded as aphrodisiacs. The ancient Greeks gave them the captivating name Golden Apples of Cydonia (a town in Crete) and treated quince as a symbol of love and fertility. In perhaps the first version of confetti, dozens of ripe fruits were tossed from chariots when couples triumphantly rode through town after tying the knot. Greek brides were also expected to nibble on quince, which has a delicious fragrance, before entering the bridal chamber. Perfuming their kisses was the general idea. However, let's hope the sweet young things got to sup on a spoonful of honey too, because uncooked quince is so astringent it can make you gag.

the ROUNDABOUT STORY of THE REAL LOVE APPLE

It was, believe it or not, a tomato. The French—trust them— came up with the name *pomme d'amour* after Columbus and his cronies brought tomatoes back to Europe from the New World. Eating the globular, juicy fruits (which we now technically regard as vegetables) struck the well-to-do in Paris as a perfect prelude to bouts in the boudoir.

But was it love at first bite for the conquistadors too? No way, José. Although the plants originated in Peru, tomatoes were discovered in Mexico, where Nahuatl Indians called them *tomatl*, but the Spanish initially refused to eat them, presuming the plants were poisonous. As French murmurings about love apples spread throughout Europe, that perception eventually changed, yet tomatoes won the hearts of Italians primarily because of their taste. An Italian doctor and botanist, Pietro

Andrea Matthiola, dubbed them *Mala aurea*—or golden apple—because tomatoes back then were an orangey-yellow colour, not red. Like dietitians today who trumpet the benefits of lyco-pene in tomatoes, the good *dottore* also thought they could be beneficial to health.

Love Potion Number 10

Peel an apple. Coddle it in your armpit until the fruit is infused with your scent. Then present this "love apple" to your lover. Eating an apple on your wedding night will also enhance fertility. MEDIEVAL BELIEF

The third U.S. president, Thomas Jefferson, fell for the strange New World fruit too. A keen plantsman who relished trying anything new (he was partly responsible for populariz-ing tulips in North America), Jefferson grew tomatoes at his home in Monticello, Virginia, as early as 1781 and encouraged early colonial settlers to do the same. At about the same time, back in Europe, the first recipe for that utterly irresistible combination—tomatoes served with pasta—was being invented by a nobleman called Ippolito Cavalcanti, Duke of Buonvicino.

The Aztec anomaly settled firmly into the Old World, it then came back to the New World with the mass immigration of Italians, who toted tomato recipes and seeds along in their luggage. A German gent called Henry J. Heinz also played a part with his novelty invention that he called catsup. Today, every American consumes about 22 pounds of tomatoes a year—mostly as bottled tomato sauce or as that ubiquitous companion to hamburgers and French fries that we now know as ketchup.

It's hardly a romantic end to a tale that started in the mountains of Peru. Yet the link between the tomato and love remains steadfast on one sun-kissed island in the Indian Ocean. The people of the former French colony of Mauritius still call tomatoes by the lovely name *pommes d'amour*. And *vive la différence*.

more TASTY TURN-ONS *from* THE GARDEN

Apples: Who doesn't love biting into these curvaceous, crunchy orbs, in red, green, yellow, and russet? And even if they're not the fabled fruit eaten by Adam and Eve, apples have a long association with sex. Particularly their pips. Country girls in Britain tested their lovers' fidelity by throwing a pip into the fire. If it burst, he was loyal. If it stayed whole, he was fooling around. And in another long-standing British tradition,

moms advise marriageable daughters when peeling an apple
to hold the knife in the right hand, then to pare very carefully,
so the peel stays in one piece. Tossed over the left shoulder,
this apple skin will then form the initial of their future husband when it hits the floor.

Bananas: Often the butt of jokes because of their shape, they've
also been used as a test of fidelity. One myth goes that a woman
should ask her man if he's faithful,
then cut the end off a ripe banana.
If there's a Y shape in the centre
of the fruit where the seeds are,
she can relax. A black blob? He's
cheating on you, dear.

Durians: Don't take a durian on the
subway in Singapore or you'll be arrested. This weird big
green spiky fruit has such an unbearable stink (said to
be an amalgam of garlic, compost, and rancid cheese)
it's banned from public transit. Yet the irony is durians
are decidedly different if you eat them. Legions of
admirers in Asia say the custardy flesh tastes like "a
combination of vanilla, caramel, and bananas, with
a touch of onion" and claim that consuming the stuff
turns them on. In fact, Malaysians have an expression,
"When the durians come down, the sarongs come off."

Your tongue finds them clitoral
as it slides up the pod.
Peas are not amused.
They have spent all their lives
keeping their knees together.

LORNA CROZIER, "PEAS"

Fava or broad beans: These flattish oval beans hardly seem sexy. Yet beliefs abound about their ability to arouse both men and women. "There is no lustier scent than a beanfield in bloom" goes one saying. There's also this painful piece of advice dispensed in Suffolk, England, to a frustrated farm lad: "Take har into a bin field, boy, and if there's a thorn bush or bit o' barbed wire, back her up agin it and she'll keep a' comin' farrad to ye." The origin of this salty sentiment isn't known. Nor is the girl's reaction.

Hazelnuts: Hints of sinister sex here. In Britain, young girls were warned that if they went off collecting hazelnuts, they'd wind up "lying down in some shady grove" and getting knocked up. And if they decided to go nutting on Sunday, disaster. They'd get the devil for a lover.

Lychees: Whitish fleshy fruits with big, shiny seeds, once only available canned in North America. Nowadays, though, city greengrocers and Asian supermarkets sell fresh lychees in little bunches—and peeling the hard, nubbly skin off one and popping it into your own mouth (or a lover's) has a sort of seductive charm. Chinese emperors

thought so too. They gave bunches of lychees to their concubines to keep them happy.

Love Potion Number 11

Green peas boiled carefully with onions and powdered with
cinnamon, ginger and cardamom create for the consumer
amorous passion and strength in coitus.

SHEIKH NEFZAWI, *THE PERFUMED GARDEN*

Mangoes: Men in India are sometimes prescribed "mango therapy" to improve their virility. This fruit is said to be high in
nutrients that can launch lagging libidos into the stratosphere.
And the Hindu love bible, the *Kama Sutra*, recommends performing a certain sexual act as if you are sucking on a mango.

Oats: Porridge sexy? Yes, in bygone days. The expression "sowing
your wild oats" originated in the Middle East, where oatmeal
was considered an aphrodisiac. To Scots and Germans, it has
also long been a symbol of hardiness, strength, and virility.

Oranges: These were rare, expensive, and highly prized during
China's Sun Dynasty, when cutting open and sharing a ripe,
juicy orange was a custom of courting couples. Then after
making love for the first time, couples would bathe together
in orange-scented rosewater to ensure "a passionate union."

Papaya: On the Caribbean island of Cuba, this orange-fleshed tropical fruit with black seeds is called *fruta bomba* because of its reputation as an aphrodisiac. And *papaya* is a Cuban slang word used to describe a woman's private parts.

Peaches: How cheeky. The fuzz that adorns their buttock-like curves is called—fittingly—"pubescence." Eating peaches before sex is a rite in some cultures. The same goes for apricots. In Japan, on Peach Blossom Day, young girls decorate their homes with flowers of peach trees in order to ensure happiness in marriage.

Strawberries: Symbols of Venus to the ancient Romans, they are favourites in erotic literature and visual art. English poet Edmund Spenser wrote that a woman's bosom was "lyke a strawberry bed." And in *The Garden of Earthly Delights*, a famous painting by Dutch artist Hieronymus Bosch, naked men and women cavort around gigantic Disneyland-ish strawberries. To enhance their lovemaking, newlyweds in rural France were once served strawberry soup on their wedding night.

Walnuts: Rutting Romans gobbled lots of walnuts, calling them *Jovis glans*, or "the glans of Jupiter" (the glans is the rounded tip of the penis). But nowadays, watch for walnuts to replace Viagra. A University of Malaya professor has come up with a "walnut pill" that works wonders for men suffering from erectile dysfunction and is said to have no harmful side effects.

LUST

THE ORCHID
The flower that drives men mad

If a horticultural association ever decided to hold a contest for the world's most erotic plants—and, indeed, why not?—which kind would win?

Orchids. Almost certainly orchids. They'd likely walk off with all the honours, in every category (especially if most of the folks doing the voting were men).

Sensuous. Mysterious. Enticing. Hypnotic. Breathtakingly beautiful. Sometimes grotesque. And as sexually in-your-face as that famous lolling red tongue of the Rolling Stones' logo.

Orchids are all of those things. And more. These flowers, of which there's a staggering number and variety—at least 30,000 species, at last count—exert such a hold over humans, they have actually driven men mad with desire. Countless true stories are told about early explorers who risked their necks hunting for orchids in tropical jungles. They tramped through fetid swamps, clambered up enormous trees, broke their legs in traps set for wild animals, contracted dysentery and malaria, were attacked by indignant natives, and when their elusive prey—usually a particular species of orchid—couldn't be found, a few fell into such depths of depression that they contemplated suicide.

All for a flower.

It's a peculiar, neurotic kind of fascination, which continues unabated today. Modern Indiana Joneses still scour the globe in search of new species of orchids. Collectors still compete fiercely to buy their booty— often in secret. (Orchid smuggling is now a hot issue, with many countries banning the har- vesting of wild species.) And it's been going on for hundreds of years.

Is our fascination with orchids sexual? Partly, for sure. Just watch the reaction of spectators at orchid shows. If they haven't seen the flowers before, there's a fair bit of sniggering and whispering behind cupped hands when people notice, for the first time, the blatantly explicit way many orchids show off their sexual organs.

Occasionally, an embar- rassed gale of laughter will echo around the exhibit hall too, because, after all, their genital embellishments often do resemble our own—in a startlingly obvious way. Yet, for orchid fanciers—who are mostly male— this obsession seems to be an unspoken kind of love. Perhaps sexual in origin, but also deeply personal, kept under wraps, and rarely voiced outside the closed, rather insular world of orchid collecting and breeding. In fact, if a contest for erotic flowers were held, orchids would probably garner top spot only if participants cast their votes in secret.

Perhaps their extraordinary allure is impossible to put into words, because those who adore orchids find it hard to explain why. And most of the addicted do shy away from an erotic connection even though a few of the plants they're passionate about sport names like 'Sabot of Venus,' 'Lady of the Night,' and 'Thunder Thighs.' (Yes, really. It's a kind of *Paphiopedilum*.) Authors of books on growing these notoriously difficult flowers also avoid the nitty-gritty of probing into exactly why they prompt so many otherwise sane men (and some women) to such heights of ecstasy.

Not so in the past, though. Ancient cultures relished the sexually charged aura of orchids—and they weren't shy about saying so.

NYMPHS *and* SATYRS COME OUT *to* PLAY

In the language of flowers, orchids have several noble meanings—a message of love, beauty, wisdom, thoughtfulness, and mature charm. (The latter refers to the *Cattleya* species of orchids, which middle-aged ladies used to wear as corsages—certainly appropriate, in view of their symbolism.) The early Greeks were, however, more down to earth. The word *Orchis* derives from their word for testicles—and it's clear why that name came about. The roots of wild orchid species are equipped with a pair of oval tubers that look remarkably like male private parts. Over the years, and in many countries, these tubers have been accorded nicknames like dogstones, hare's bollocks, and sweet cods— presumably in a reference to the saucy bundles of stuffing, called codpieces, that Elizabethan men used to shove into their trousers to amplify a crucial area of their anatomy.

Love Potion Number 12

Dip an orchid tuber in wine, then hold it in your hand.
This will ignite sexual desire.

PLINY THE ELDER, GREEK PHILOSOPHER

Sex is front and centre, too, in old myths about orchids. In one Greek myth, Orchis was born to a nymph called Acolasia and the satyr Patellanus. Theirs was a union of countless hot nights. Passion gripped them constantly. Then their handsome son Orchis developed a liking for the sprightly side of life too. He presided over feasts for Priapus (the god who gave rise to the name of the painful state of constant arousal that can send modern men who've overdone the Viagra rushing to emergency departments). But Orchis, naughty boy, got a bit carried away at one bash. After letting his hands wander all over an out-of-bounds mortal priestess, he was promptly torn to pieces by the gods. So grieving Pa Patellanus transformed his son's remains into an orchid flower.

But in another version of this myth, Orchis gets left out of the fun and games. Instead, the "uncontrollable copulations" of Patellanus are said to have spilled onto the ground and given rise to the first orchid ever, named Satyrion in his honour. Then Dioscorides, a Greek physician who was around in first century AD, added fuel to the flame by writing in his *Materia Medica* that orchids were a definite sex aid. Men should eat their roots, he decreed, to determine the gender of their offspring. Large, testicle-shaped tubers resulted in boys, while slimmer, slighter ones would lead to the birth of girls.

Meanwhile, continents away in China, the orchid had a less risqué image. Regarded as one of the Four Gentlemen in the world of flowers (the others are plum blossom, bamboo, and chrysanthemums), orchids represented the virtues of the perfectly cultured male—that is, integrity, humility, and refinement. Yet a soupçon of sex was clearly in the cards for this paragon of good behaviour. The Chinese word for orchid is *lan*, and in the *Shi-ching* (*Book of Poems*), supposedly edited by Confucius, there's a conversation between a couple about the possibility of going somewhere to make love. The man is hesitant (perhaps worried about his gentlemanly status) but the woman has no such concerns. The poem goes, in part, like this:

> And men and women of the state wear *lan* now
> She says again: There let us go
> There is a place beyond the river Yu
> Where we can our love do . . .

The link between orchids and sexual desire is omnipresent throughout history—even if, today, we choose to discount it.

WHICH *are* THE WORLD'S SEXIEST ORCHIDS?

That's debatable, but many people plump for the *Paphiopedilum* species. Called "paphs" (pronounced paffs) by collectors, they're known commonly as slipper orchids, because their dominant characteristic is a plump, bulging, voluptuous pouch (called the labellum) that sort of resembles a little Cinderella–like shoe. This strange appendage sits—apparently suspended in mid-air—in front of petals that spread themselves provocatively wide and, in some species, look like freckled human skin. Then at the centre of this whole rather suggestive set-up, there's a "tongue" protruding from a tight crevice, ornamented some-times with a little clitoral knob.

Paphs are among the favourites of Michelle Wan, author of four best-selling novels (including one called *Deadly Slipper*) about orchid intrigue and skulduggery in the Dordogne area of France. And she's one of the few orchid fanciers to admit that she does find their appearance erotic.

"Frankly, the heavy veining in the labellum of some species, like *Cypripedium tibeticum*, which is dark purple and swollen, does put one in mind of testicles," she says, with a chuckle. Sure does.

Paphs originated in the tropics. But the *Cypripedium* species, which are a sub-group in the *Paphiopedilum* family, grow wild in northern climates, and they can be, as Wan says, every bit as licentious-looking as their southern cousins. Indeed their name comes from the Greek *Kypris pedion*, which loosely translates as "the genital region of Aphrodite." In one kind, *Cypripedium acaule*, the pouch is raspberry pink (hence its common name, pink lady slipper), and it comes equipped with a provocative little slit at the front. Another more common kind, *Cypripedium calceolatus*, sports a yellow pouch and brown side petals that hang down like ribbons and wave in the wind. Both used to be common in North America and still

My lover fragrant as incense
Adjusts my jade hairpins, and
Draws on my silk stockings
Over my feet and legs
Perfumed with orchids
And once again we fall over
Overwhelmed with passion

HUANG E, "TO THE TUNE OF 'A FLOATING CLOUD CROSSES ENCHANTED MOUNTAIN'" flourish in a few locations (sadly, that's not the case in the U.K., where *C. calceolatus* is now considered virtually extinct). They like acid soil that's fairly damp and are usually found in partly shaded places that were once cultivated but now aren't, like an overgrown field or logged regrowth area of pines and spruce.

You need the eyes of a hawk to spot them, though—and Michelle Wan suggests a novel way of doing it (for females, that is): "Crouch down and have a pee," she recommends. "That's when you tend to notice orchids, because they're often partly hidden in long grass and other foliage." The flowers appear in late spring and, typical of all orchids, last a long time. They're pretty little charmers, too. In fact, stumbling across a treasure trove of *Cypripedium* while answering the call of nature is enough to make hearts flutter—whether you find them erotic-looking or not.

Love Potion Number 13

Cut twenty stems from the Early Purple Orchid *Orchis mascula*. Squeeze out the nectar into warm goat's milk or yoghurt and drink the liquid. This hath great force to provide the desire for coition and doth egregiously excite both sexes therewith.

JOHN PARTRIDGE, PHYSICIAN TO CHARLES I OF ENGLAND

why ORCHIDS *are* SUCH SHAMELESS SHOW-OFFS

Pseudo-copulation. It sounds like some kind of therapy at a sex clinic in California. Yet this is the word botanists use to describe the devious way plants trick insects into fertilizing their flowers—and orchids are very, very good at it.

Out of necessity. It's a frustrating and anxious business, being an orchid. Most members of this complicated plant family can't reproduce on their own. They need an intimate partner in the pollination process. And being rooted to the spot where they grow, it isn't possible for them to just drop everything and go tromping off through the woods, looking for a suitable candidate. The truth is, orchids—like humans—often have to wait an awfully long time for "Mr. Right" to come along.

This need to play the waiting game is the reason why blooms on some species of orchids last for months. They deck themselves out in winsome petals ornamented with alluring bits and bobs (making sure the whole package is tough enough to withstand damaging sun, wind, and rain) and sometimes throw in come-hither scents for good measure. Then they just sit tight, proudly posing in their finery, hungry for sex, and no doubt doing a plant's version of crossing their fingers, in the hopes of wooing that all-important suitor to their side.

Who's the lucky fellow? Usually a bee, wasp, or fly. But butterflies, beetles, bats, night-flying moths, sometimes birds,
and even small mammals like mice might be enlisted in the
carnal manoeuvring that's part of the pollination ritual for
flowers like orchids. And they sure know how to tease these
suitors with erotic foreplay. Their *modus operandi* is to con any
unsuspecting twerps who land on their petals into thinking
they're going to get it on, when in reality all that will happen is
that the visitors' frenzied movements will enable the orchid
flowers to fertilize one another and thus reproduce seeds. It's
deception on a grand scale. But it sure does work.

Some shining examples of orchid deceit:

Bee orchid *Ophrys apifera*: The centre of this flower looks exactly
like a plump little furry female bee. And deliberately so.
When a gullible male bee stops by and tries to mate with
his new-found lady love, during his vigorous humping, the
shiny yellow pollen mass of the flower detaches itself and
sticks to his undercarriage. But the bee orchid is a bit of
a tease because she thwarts her partner's urge to climax.
Crazy with frustration, he moves on to another orchid and
tries again. And in doing so, the bee rubs the pollen off his
stomach onto the moist, concave stigma. And bingo. The
bee orchid race will survive for another generation.

Mirror orchid *Ophrys speculum*: A lusty little harlot with a protruding lip that glints like a blue metallic mirror, with a fringe of reddish hairs. Such equipment (and the rest of its wardrobe) is designed to exactly mimic a female digger wasp *Camposcolia ciliata*. And the male diggers sure dig the message.

Peruvian bucket orchid *Coryanthes mastersiana*: Drawn to this flower by its fragrance, a hapless male bee falls feet first into a "bucket" full of water—in reality, a cup-like petal—picking up pollen on its back along the way. With its wings wet, flying out is impossible, so the bee climbs through a tight-fitting hatch to escape, but struggles so much, the loose pollen grains clinging to its back get transferred to the sticky stigma, the female part of the flower.

Trichoceros antennifera: Popular in southern California, this orchid, which has no common name, is grown out of doors in gardens. And it is pollinated by a fly with the tongue-twisting name *Paragymnomma*. The lip and centre of the orchid look identical to the female fly of the species, and thus they lure the male into getting himself into a lather on the flower's pollen mass. Then he flies off to another flower and, like other bees that have been similarly deceived, leaves this "gift" behind.

Yellow orchid *Ophrys lutea*: A fairly common species that grows on the shores of the Mediterranean, it is equipped with a lip that looks (to a male bee) like a female bee lying head down on the flower, with her bottom in the air. Enough said.

the DRACULA ORCHID

For those who lean toward the dark side of sexual desire, this orchid sure makes a good companion.

The name *Dracula* actually means "little dragon," which sounds pretty harmless, yet the varieties sporting names like *Dracula nosferatu, Dracula diabola,* and *Dracula vampira* would be right at home in a Christopher Lee movie. Indeed, the flowers of most dracs (as they are known in the horticultural trade) are creepily erotic and often have weird "faces" and a decidedly sensual tongue lolling out at the centre. Their murky colour combinations can be offbeat too, hinting at devilish deeds done after the clock strikes twelve. And, fittingly, they prefer lurking in the shadows, away from direct sunlight.

Yet in spite of these sinister overtones, dracs are an example of the kind of orchids that exert a strange power over those who see them. You can't help being drawn to the flowers, while perhaps shuddering inwardly at the same time.

The biggest fan of this odd branch of the orchid family was an eccentric Brit with the long-winded name of Schomberg Henry Kerr, 9th Marquess of Lothian. At the turn of the twentieth century, his *Dracula chimaera* was the first of its kind to flower in England—and it caused an immediate sensation among plant collectors. It's not hard to see why, either. *Chimaera* now means "monstrous" in horticultural Latin, but it's also the name of a terrifying, dragon-like creature that people once thought existed and was supposedly discovered by Satan. And the orchid flowers with this title certainly live up to their namesake's legendary image. Vaguely triangular in shape in most drac species, they look a bit like dragons come down to earth. Petals are a mix of cream and grey, with maroon splotches and strange, slim "tails" hanging down their sides. When fully extended, these tails turn the bloom into one of the world's biggest and most extraordinary looking orchids, measuring about 15 inches wide from tip to tip.

Although their native habitat is Central and South America, dracs—unlike many other tropical orchids—like things cool and grow in mountainous regions where the thermometer plummets once the sun goes down. If it's too warm, a vampire orchid won't come out at night to play. It will simply droop—and give up the ghost.

the VANILLA ORCHID

It's been scientifically proven that guys get turned on by the smell of vanilla. Females, however, are said to be more titillated by the taste. Either way, the pleasurable sensation both sexes derive from this flavouring comes courtesy of an orchid—the only orchid, in fact, that produces edible fruit.

Love Potion Number 14

For a romantic evening:
An arrangement of *Dendrobium* orchid sprays, for the eyes
Vanilla-scented candles, for the nose
Chocolates served with vanilla tea, for the taste buds
Massage oil with vanilla extract, for touch
Your favourite romantic music, for the ears

AUSTRALIAN ORCHID COUNCIL

There are more than sixty species of these orchids growing around the globe, all in tropical regions, but the kind that's now mostly used in food is *Vanilla planifolia*. And as orchids go, it's not exactly a looker. Small and lily-like, the greenish-white flowers appear up and down a nondescript vine that snakes up tree trunks in the tropics. These blooms have the "hibiscus habit"; they open wide for only one day before closing themselves up again and withering away. The vanilla pod is where the action is—but it takes its sweet time getting there. The development period of pods is actually as long as that of a human baby (from eight to ten months) and even when they're long, green, plump, and ripe for picking, the pods still have a long way to go before becoming the exquisite like-nothing-else taste that we adore. (Always add a teaspoonful of pure vanilla essence when you make cakes, bakers say—and they're right. The sensual flavour makes the most ordinary of baked goods taste divinely expensive.)

Vanilla pods are sauna addicts: they need many complicated rounds of sweating, drying, then sweating again before they're ready to face the world as a flavouring. It's a process that can take months (something to remember, the next time you balk at paying six dollars for a single dried, black pod sold in a glass tube). Yet even though the preparation process is arduous and labour-intensive, humans have been willingly undertaking the task for centuries—and one reason (at least in the past) was vanilla's magical link with sex.

The plants originated in Mexico, where Montezuma is reputed to have consumed copious amounts of vanilla in a chocolate drink before making love to his wives. Before him, Totonac Indians told a legend about Princess Xanat, the pretty young daughter of the Mexican fertility god, Opochtli. It was Xanat's misfortune to fall in love with a Totonac youth, but her father forbade them to marry, because the youth was mortal and she wasn't. So the lovers fled to the jungle with Dad in hot pursuit, and when he caught them, he chopped their heads off. (Most flower legends are, alas, on the gruesome side.) Then in the spot where their blood dribbled onto the ground, the first vanilla orchid grew.

The Totonacs called this flower *tlilxo-chitl* or "black flower" because the big seed pod it produced after flowering surprised them by turning black. Then testosterone-fuelled Cortes and his crew came along. After hearing about the plant's aphrodisiacal power from Montezuma (and no doubt shagging a few of his women), the invaders from Spain gave it the name *vainilla,* meaning "little pocket" or "sheath" in Spanish—a description that was undoubtedly chosen because *vaina* also happens to mean "vagina" in Latin.

The lusty conquistadors fell head over heels in love with vanilla, perhaps influenced by its purported side effects. They prized it as much as the gold, silver, and jewellery they kept plundering from the New World. They also took the plants every-where they travelled, with the result that most of the world's vanilla crop is now cultivated in Madagascar, not Mexico. And here's the irony. As a consequence of their zeal, vanilla has become so widely used that the term "plain vanilla" is now regarded as something of an insult. More's the pity. Honest-to-goodness plain vanilla essence (not the awful artificial kind, known as vanillin) is surely unequalled by any other kind of flavouring, particularly in ice cream and cakes. And it all comes to us courtesy of an ordinary little orchid.

LIKENED *to* COURTESANS *by* A FAMOUS PLAYWRIGHT

Perhaps more than any other flower, orchids tweak our senses, arousing strong opinions. Arguments for or against them can get pretty heated, because there's rarely a middle ground. Fans have included Aztec emperor Montezuma, Captain William Bligh (of Mutiny on the Bounty fame), Raymond Burr (better known as TV detective Perry Mason), Francis Drake (acolyte of Queen Elizabeth I), the current Queen Elizabeth, crime writer Agatha Christie, and playwright George Bernard Shaw, who was intrigued by orchids' "sexual apparatus" and likened them to courtesans.

> [Orchids are] nasty things. Their flesh is too much like the flesh of men, and their perfume has the rotten sweetness of corruption.
>
> GENERAL STERNWOOD, FROM THE FILM *The Big Sleep*

And the detractors? French novelist Marcel Proust couldn't decide whether he liked orchids or not and compared the flowers to "harlots and homosexuals." But Victorian poet and art critic John Ruskin was unequivocal in his dislike. Horrified by orchids' overt sexuality, he called them "prurient apparitions."

the WORLD'S TASTIEST APHRODISIAC?

Forget Viagra. If your love life is flagging, dip into a dish of orchid ice cream. Things will almost certainly perk up.

This is no joke. *Salepi dondurma* is a treat served in ice-cream shops in Turkey. It comes in over thirty delicious flavours such as pistachio nut and apricot, it has a firmer texture than regular ice cream, and Turkish men claim that it can definitely "strengthen the body" with emphasis—wink, wink—on a certain area below the belt.

This unique delicacy is made from the dried, tuberous roots of wild orchids. Villagers dig up the tubers in the mountains of the Anatolia region during spring and summer. The tubers are then dispatched to Turkey's capital, Istanbul, where mills grind the roots into a whitish translucent flour called *salep*. This flour, which has a gluey texture when wet, is mixed with milk, sugar, and various flavourings, beaten to a smooth consistency with metal rods, and served in little glass dessert dishes.

Another surprise: the Turks' answer to Ben and Jerry's

Chunky Monkey tastes every bit as good as conventional ice cream. Just ask Eric Hansen, author of the illuminating book *Orchid Fever: A Horticultural Tale of Love, Lust and Lunacy.* Hansen travelled to Turkey to verify the existence of this quirky boost to the libido and came away convinced of one thing: aphrodisiac or not, it tastes truly yummy. He even took a bag of *salep* flour home to San Francisco so he could make his own orchid ice cream.

As for its ability to strengthen the "body," well, why not? After all, the word *salep* comes from the Arabic *sahlab*, which means "testicles of the fox." And if you examine the orchid tubers used to make this unusual ice cream—which all belong to the *Orchis* family and include species such as *O. latifolia, O. mascula, O. maculata,* and *O. anatolica*—they bear a striking resemblance to human male anatomy. Then, remember that name *Orchis*? Yes, testicles again.

Two explicit references to the male sex in one delicious dessert. Wow. Whatever the truth, orchid ice cream sounds a whole lot more exciting to share with a lover than a bowl of Baskin Robbins.

Mandragora mas.
Mandragore.

DENIAL

THE MANDRAKE
The unsavoury obsession of a celebrity nun

Hildegard von Bingen. The name probably rings a bell with most of us. And her fame is remarkable, really, because this Benedictine nun died nearly a thousand years ago. Yet here we are, in the twenty-first century, and once-forgotten Hildegard has catapulted right out of her tomb and become a sort of Princess Diana of the Middle Ages. Feminist scholars set her on the road to celebrity status about a decade ago, when they began unearthing her haunting music, her miniature illumi-nated manuscripts (which are exquisite for their design sense alone), and her long-winded musings about God, nature, and botanical medicine. Now images of this strong-jawed woman in a nun's wimple (who's depicted as looking a bit like the actress Vanessa Redgrave) keep popping up everywhere.

There seems no end, in fact, to the barrage of Bingen-inspired ballyhoo. She is hailed as a visionary, saint, and general do-gooder by everyone from eco-evangelists to gardeners to champions of women's rights. It all just goes to show that it's never too late for someone to become famous.

Yet, like many celebrities, Hildegard had a dark side. She was obsessed with one topic. Sex. Or rather, she hated the whole idea of it and made strenuous efforts to ensure that everybody else thought the same way. While abbess of a priory in Eibingen, Germany, she wrote about the evils of physical longings and nagged the nubile young nuns under her control about how allowing such thoughts to enter their heads was tantamount to inviting Satan in. And her biggest weapon in this battle was plants. All kinds of plants.

According to plant historian Alec Bristow, Hildegard relished making anti-sex potions from herbs that grew in the nunnery garden. She compiled lists of potential ingredients—roots, foliage, flowers, seeds, anything, really—that she thought could, in various combinations, put the lid on libido. She wasn't alone in this preoccupation, of course. Religious communities of both sexes were constantly on the lookout for ways to stop their members from entertaining unseemly fantasies. In fact, they aimed to make the whole idea of sex so utterly revolting, no one would ever want to think about it at all. And practically speaking, this philosophy made sense. After all, everyone in those closeted communities had pledged to stay celibate, and what Mother Superior wanted to deal with a lot of carnal carrying-on in her cloisters?

So seeking purity in thought and deed, church officialdom resorted to some disgusting measures to ensure lifelong celibacy. Their favourite tactic was inflicting foul-smelling substances on offenders. Think rotten eggs blended with onions, henna flowers, and the ground-up roots of a common garden plant called mallow. Novitiate nuns and monks were ordered to spread this all over their bodies and not wash it off for weeks, until presumably the "malady" that afflicted them was conquered. Other concoctions had to be swallowed.

Hildegard seems to have got particularly hot and bothered about mandrake root. She banished it from the nunnery garden, and many of her anaphrodisiac mixtures (the opposite of aphrodisiacs) were designed to destroy the "ill effects of this evil weed." One involved the roots of perennial geraniums (now popular and thoroughly inoffensive occupants of our gardens) mashed with shoots of broom until they formed a thick paste. A naughty nun would be commanded to lie down on her pallet as her skirts were pushed up over her head. Then other nuns would smear Hildegard's repellent remedy all over her private parts.

Did these concoctions quell the feelings of Sister Dagmar for Sister Mary Margaret? Or, for that matter, for Father Martin, who made many a maidenly heart flutter when he came over to the nunnery to officiate at Matins? Well, maybe. But if the offending nuns and brothers stayed on the straight and narrow as a consequence of these potions, it was more likely out of fear and guilt rather than the lust-limiting effect of the plants themselves. Of course, there's also the possibility that they stank so much, no one wanted to go near them.

And the ironical aspect of Hildegard of Bingen's ascent to virtual sainthood today is that she recently acquired the nickname "Sibyll of the Rhine." A sibyll? Hardly. This dragon lady was no lusty siren crooning come-hither stanzas beside Germany's biggest river. In fact, if she were around today, we probably wouldn't lionize her. We'd rush her off to the nearest therapist.

THE MIGHT *of* THE MANDRAKE
Mandragora officinarum

Mysterious. Magical. The stuff of witches' brews, wet dreams, and things that go hump in the night. Mandrake has long been a key player—albeit a dubious one—in the erotic garden of delights.

And it's all because of the way this plant grows. A member of the nightshade family, it develops forked roots that are impressively long (up to 4 feet) and heavy (4 or 5 pounds) and that bear a vague resemblance to the human body. In Hildegard von Bingen's day, people believed that there were two kinds of mandrake, male and female: the male had a third (and smaller) root hanging down between his forked "legs" while the females possessed a slit in the same spot. As a result, men were supposed to cut up the "male plants" and eat them, while their womenfolk nibbled on the "females."

Why? Well, this unpalatable-sounding snack served a definite purpose. Procreation. The roots apparently had the sure-fire ability to make people fertile—a belief that crops up in the Bible. In the Book of Genesis there's a complex tale about two sisters, Leah and Rachel, who are married to the same man, Jacob. Although Leah has given him many children, Jacob prefers Rachel (who is barren) and spends a lot of time with her, arousing Leah's ire. The bitter rivals strike a deal when one of Leah's brood finds some mandrake roots and gives it to her. Leah lets Rachel eat the roots too, in return for being allowed to return to Jacob's bed for one more night. And such is the force of their "medicine" that both women subsequently become pregnant, to the delight of all.

But this plant isn't simply credited with helping wives conceive. Cultures around the world have used its supposedly magical powers with less amicable purposes in mind. There is a famous story about the Carthaginian general Hannibal feigning retreat from African troops and leaving behind large quantities of wine adulterated with mandrake roots. The Africans got plastered on the wine and fell asleep for hours as Hannibal snuck back to defeat them. Even so, the plant's prime value throughout history has

Give me to drink mandragora . . .
That I might sleep out this great gap of time
My Antony is away.

SHAKESPEARE,
Antony and Cleopatra

been as an adjunct to sex—and a dark one at that. Machiavelli wrote a play called *Mandragola* (*The Mandrake*) in 1518, whose plot revolves around a nobleman called Callimaco who uses the plant as a sort of date-rape drug to get Lucrezia, who is married to someone else, into bed. And in an even darker twist, people throughout Europe once held the ghastly belief that mandrake would grow only where the semen of a hanged man had dripped onto the ground—surely the most unpleasant image that a plant has ever had the misfortune to be saddled with.

However, this much-maligned, supposed "monster" of Mother Nature has, in recent years, undergone something of a make-over in the image department. Its contorted roots are now regarded as a good luck charm to promote fertility in some countries bordering the Mediterranean, where the plant grows like a weed. Hang up a sexy-looking piece of root above a marriage bed, local sentiment goes, and babies are bound to follow. So dug-up roots, brushed free of dirt and looking rather like misshapen parsnips, are sometimes sold at country markets.

As for the act of digging mandrake up, here's where the story takes a decidedly painful turn. Because the plant's roots somewhat resemble the human body, people once presumed that it would scream in pain if anyone tried to pull those roots out of the ground. Thus, if a woman wanted the mandrake's assistance in conceiving, a complex and horrid procedure had to be observed. You could get the garden spade out only at night and on a Friday—designated the Day of Venus (or Day of Love). And while the plant would cooperatively glow in the dark like a lantern to reveal its location, the lady in question mustn't personally touch the leaves or stem. Lordy, no. She was supposed to stand back and stuff her pretty little ears with something in order to muffle the mandrake's "piercing cry" during its removal from the earth, because if she did hear it scream, she

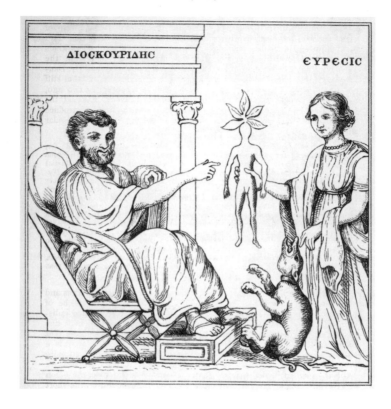

was doomed to die herself. Instead, a starving dog—yes, man's best friend—had to be tied to the plant with a rope and be persuaded to yank hard till the long roots were eased out. If Fido objected (and likely he did), the woman was to whip him into being more cooperative. And if he expired as a result of the whipping, another canine had to be called in to take over until the dastardly deed was done.

Let's hope, for the dog's sake, that the ladies weren't working with clay soil.

Not a nice tale. And there's more. Participants also had to contend with the apparent stink of mandrake. Holding their breath while this nocturnal escapade was going on was deemed necessary, because the roots' odour was "enough to knock a man down." (In reality, that's a gross exaggeration.) Shakespeare alludes to this odour and the complicated business of digging mandrake up in *Romeo and Juliet* when he writes:

What with loathesome smells
And shrikes like mandrakes
torn out of the earth
That living mortals, hearing them, run mad.

PUTTING MANDRAKE on THE MENU TODAY

In a word, don't. Shakespeare thought eating the roots was likely to induce nothing more than a long, drugged sleep. He alludes to this in no less than four of his plays, most notably when the friar makes Juliet drink a potion brewed from "mandragora" after her secret wedding to Romeo, so that she will fall into a death-like slumber. Yet to susceptible individuals, particularly children, this plant can be very bad news. It contains the same poisonous properties as its more commonly seen relative, deadly nightshade *Atropa belladonna*. This unruly, climbing weed flourishes in uncultivated areas all over the world and sometimes invades our gardens with its tenacious tangle of roots. Tots are irresistibly drawn to its delectable-looking, but potentially deadly, bunches of bright scarlet berries, which grow on the twining stems in late summer. These should never be eaten. Nor should the berries clustered on its cousin.

TWO *other* PRIAPIC PERFORMERS

Ginseng looks a lot like mandrake—the roots, that is. So it's no surprise that this well-known herb (which the Chinese call *Jin-chen*, meaning "man-like") has an arousing reputation in the bedchamber too. Thought to heal all parts of the body, it's now familiar around the world as a general aid to health. Yet back in the 1600s, ginseng was better known as an aphrodisiac—and the more its roots resembled the human body, the more valuable they were. The Dutch brought the roots to Europe from the Far East. One French king, Louis XIV, reportedly found their effect "very beneficial."

But lusty Louis would have been well advised to steer clear

of the seductive charms of a plant called *Solanum sodomeum*. It's yet another member of the multi-faceted nightshade family and grows wild along the Mediterranean seashore. And on a hot sunny afternoon, its shiny, yellowish fruits can look quite munchable and thirst-quenching. Yet watch out. This plant has the common name of apple of Sodom, and with a moniker like that, it is—no surprise—imbued with a reputation of precipitating all kinds of carnal hanky-panky.

Ancient travellers returning to Europe from what is now the Middle East reportedly saw this *Solanum* growing in abundance in Sodom and Gomorrah, the twin biblical cities that God is supposed to have destroyed by fire because of their citizens' wicked ways. The plant lures people to it, the legend goes, with the mouth-watering appearance of its fruits, which have the ability to inspire "unspeakable" acts. Yet the moment anyone tries to pick them, the little orbs dissolve into smoke and ashes—God's way of warning us that we could suffer the same fate as the sinners who lived in Sodom and Gomorrah. How did this bizarre belief come about? The scientific explanation offered by modern botanists is that the berries were once afflicted by burrowing insect pests that attacked and ate their flesh from the inside. The fruit eventually dried out and then crumbled when touched by human hands. But whatever the real story of *Solanum sodomeum*, this plant is still regarded as a symbol of sin in some parts of the Middle East.

MANDRAKE at THE MOVIES

Dark associations with witchcraft and other hocus-pocus have made mandrake irresistible to a whole horde of novelists and movie-makers. Some of the different ways they use the weed:

- Heart-rending screams. In the book and film version of J.K. Rowling's *Harry Potter and the Chamber of Secrets*, Professor Sprout equips Harry and his pals with earmuffs to stop them hearing the mandrake howl with pain while they repot its seedlings.
- Screaming and semen. Author Salman Rushdie opts for both in his novel *The Enchantress of Florence*, in which boys try to grow mandrake using the semen of a hanged archbishop.
- More screaming. William S. Burroughs has a character called Johnny "scream like a mandrake" in *The Naked Lunch*.

PLANTS that KILL PASSION

What will halt an unstoppable mania to make love? There's always the cold shower, of course. Here are a few other options from the plant world:

Chaste tree *Vitex agnus castus*: Grows in the Mediterranean and Africa. Aromatic and quite pretty, with purple flowers. Used for centuries by male clergy (who called it "monks' pepper") and nuns as a tea to "calm unhallowed emotions." Celibate priestesses of Ceres, Roman goddess of the Earth, slept on beds made from the tree's leaves with the same purpose in mind. And this probably isn't all fanciful nonsense. Studies have shown that chaste tree reduces testosterone levels in men. It's also used to regulate hormonal imbalances in women.

Cotton *Gossypium*: Cotton develops in fluffy white balls on tall stems, which is then processed and made into clothing around the world. These appealing orbs have become such a novelty, florists now sell the stems for use in vases. In China, though, cotton is sometimes used to quell carnal appetites. The Chinese are also experimenting with *Gossypium* as a male contraceptive.

Giant hogweed *Heracleum sphondylium*: Skyscraper of a weed with big, jagged leaves. Feared and ripped out by municipalities everywhere nowadays, because its stinging juice has an effect like that of poison ivy. But if you're brave enough to pick this plant, it can apparently be brewed as a turn-off tea. (Gloves recommended.)

Lettuce *Lactuca sativa*: Attention, guys. Perhaps salad *is* for wimps after all. According to Gerard, author of the famed *Great Herbal*,

written in 1597, lettuce contains "juices that cooleth and quencheth the naturall seed if it be too much used." Yet in those days, women also chanted the mantra "Let us avoid lettuce" because it was thought to cause infertility. In Surrey, England, there's a record of lettuce heads being carefully counted—and if there were "too many" growing in a garden (the precise number isn't known), women dug them up.

Both superstitions probably originated with the myth of the Greek god Adonis. Attacked by a wild boar, he expired while lying on a bed of lettuce leaves. Yet in West Africa, lettuce has the opposite reputation. Fertility god Min is represented by this salad green; it is believed to promote fertility because the plant's milky white sap resembles semen or breast milk.

Anti-Love Potion Number 1

To repel the attentions of an unwanted suitor, buy him a potted marigold (the *Tagetes* kind, not *Calendula*). The plant's strong odour will dampen his ardour.

OLD COUNTRY BELIEF

Magnolia vine *Schizandra:* Native to Asia and commonly grown in gardens, it has attractive, reddish-pink flowers, but the berries are used to quell desire in Chinese medicine. As with many botanical remedies, however, *Schizandra* is also thought by some to be an aphrodisiac.

Marjoram *Origanum majorana*: *Mamma mia*. Say it isn't so. This summery, pungent herb imparts such an agreeable wallop in Italian cooking. Yet according to natural medicine mavens, munching on marjoram is not a good idea if you're preparing for a night of love.

Okra *Abelmoschus esculentus*: Caribbean vegetable with beautiful flowers (related to hibiscus) and novel pointy-ended fruits. When cooked in liquid, okra takes on a texture that feels horribly slimy as it slides down the throat. Perhaps that's why it's also reputed to dampen sexual desire.

Rue *Ruta graveolens*: Strong-smelling, common, and weedy herb. Useless in cooking, but monks and nuns once turned it into a desire-dampening tea.

Stinging nettles *Urtica dioica*: According to the Greeks, "to avoid lechery, take nettle seed and bray it in a mortar with pepper and temper it with honey or wine and it shall destroy it. . . ."

Strawberry *Fragaria*: Who doesn't love strawberries?

What a decadent delight, especially when shared with a lover. Yet strawberry leaves are claimed to have the opposite effect. In Ireland, mothers protecting their daughters' virtue used to brew a tea from the leaves to quell "excessive ardour" in the young virgins and their eager swains.

Vietnamese coriander *Polygonum odoratum*: Terrific alternative to regular coriander (also called cilantro) in cooking. Keep a pot on a window ledge all winter and snip leaves off as needed. But beware: Buddhist monks reportedly use this easy-to-grow herb to dampen sexual urges. Same goes for another member of the *Polygonum* family, popularly called Fo-ti.

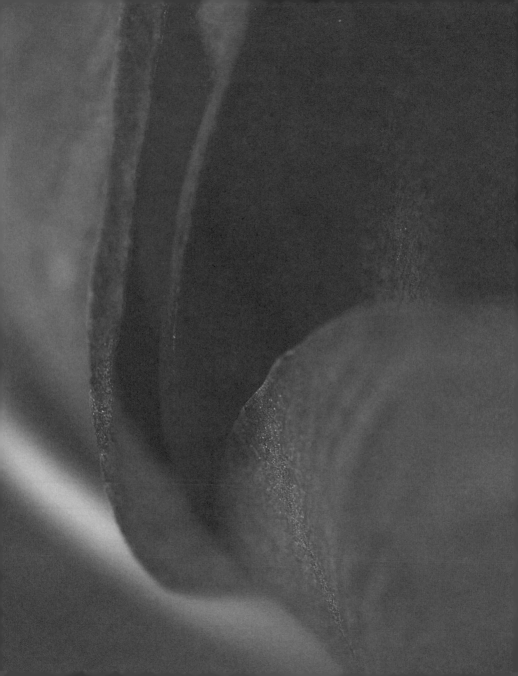

PASSION

THE TULIP
Sex symbol of the Turks

Tulips erotic? Most people would shake their heads in amazement at the suggestion. These familiar and much-loved emblems of springtime—planted more often than any other flowers on the planet—stop us in our tracks with their arresting beauty, especially after a long, hard winter. And how uplifting their striking cup-shaped blobs of colour can be, like paint daubed on a canvas, perched atop those tall, impossibly straight stems—the traffic-light reds and oranges, the sunshine yellows, the peachy and rosy pinks, the pale violet, the deep, velvety purples, the stripes of scarlet, magenta, and white. A patch of tulips suddenly sprung to life in somebody's front yard is an exhilarating jolt to the senses, because it can only mean one thing: winter is well and truly over at last.

Yet the frisson of pleasure we experience from tulips isn't sexual. Not for them the rumpled ripeness of a rose spreading her skin-like petals wide on a hot June day, nor the shameless strutting of orchids, leaving nothing to the imagination with their titillating tongues and tight little crevices, so defiantly on display at a flower show. Although the arrival of tulips signals rebirth and a year of fecund new beginnings, their demeanour is too stiff, too formal, to spark anything but a pure admiration of their austere loveliness. And when these Grace Kellys of the garden are lined up in public parks, marching soldier-like along the length of a flower bed, they can come across as truly remarkable in their uniformity of shape, size, and colour. Yet they can seem cold too. And, like the Princess of Monaco, a little too perfect. The very orderliness of tulips keeps them at a distance from us. While marvelling at the sheer proficiency of the bulbs planted in the ground below, many a fan has longed for a few of their progeny to loosen up a bit. Please, beautiful tulips, we want to say, don't be so uptight. It's okay to step out of that rigid line-up, to sprawl and kick up your legs, to flop sideways, to let your petals drop seductively open one by one, not all at the same

> The tulip is a courtly queen,
> Whom, therefore, I will shun.
>
> THOMAS HOOD, "FLOWERS"

time. Because then you'll seem warmer. Friendlier. More approachable. More like *real* flowers.

But of course the apparent coldness of tulips isn't really their fault. Rather, it stems in large measure from the way we choose to grow them. In public places, particularly, rigid rows of tulips have been customary since Victorians introduced the fashion for bedding plants laid out in neat patterns, using big swaths of single colours. And although many home gardeners are now loosening the stays of these wonderful flowers and planting them in more creative ways, that's still largely the norm today.

Not so for the early Turks, though. They regarded tulips in a vastly different light.

a ROLLICKING RELATIONSHIP *with* TULIPS

Sensual. Erotic. Definitely an instigator of carnal thoughts. For proof that tulips were once thought of in these terms, look no farther than the *Feranghiz*, the first plant catalogue in history. It was produced at the beginning of the sixteenth century for the rulers of the Ottoman empire, who were the first people to start cultivating tulips in private gardens. The catalogue wound up containing 1,588 tulip varieties to choose from (an astonishing number when you consider how long ago this happened), and they were all developed from two kinds—*Tulipa acuminata* and

Tulipa sylvestris. Rough and tough cowboys of the day discovered these spindly, original versions of modern tulips growing wild in the region of mountains and high steppes that undulates like a ribbon through what is now the Tien Shan province of China, as well as in parts of Turkey, Iran, Armenia, and Azerbaijan. The bulbs of these flowers were packed in saddlebags, then taken to be sold to the rich rulers in Constantinople (now Istanbul). The most interesting part of the catalogue is the *names* of these tulips. The Turkish sultans endowed them with lusty monikers like 'Lover's Dream,' 'Beauty's Reward,' and 'Ruby of Paradise.' There are dozens of such names. When you consider the bland,

She has the colour of the violet and the curved form of the new moon. Her markings are rightly placed, clean, and well-proportioned. Her shape is like the almond, needle-like and ornamented with pleasant rays. Her inner petals are like a well, as they should be; her outer petals are a little open, this too is as it should be. The white ornamental petals are absolutely perfect. She is the chosen of the chosen.

EARLY TURKISH DESCRIPTION OF THE PERFECT TULIP BY SHEIKH MOHAMMED

uninspiring titles that tulips are lumbered with today—think 'Apeldoorn,' 'New Design,' and 'Striped Oxford'—it's clear that this flower once had altogether far more sexy associations.

Were dour, church-dominated Dutchmen responsible for sanitizing the image of the tulip? Perhaps. They introduced the

2

flower to Europe and, subsequently, to the rest of the world. And although everyone in the Netherlands promptly went mad over this intriguing new arrival—getting caught up in bidding wars and selling everything they owned to acquire a single tulip bulb during the celebrated period of Dutch history known as Tulipomania (1623–37)—the prime motivator in the race to acquire them appears to have been the desire to make money. Purchasers didn't pursue tulips out of any particular passion for the blooms themselves. They were simply seen as a way to get rich quick.

Not so in Turkey. The Muslim sultans, unlike the Protestant Dutch, enjoyed a rollicking relationship with their tulips. They called them *Lale* and planted literally millions of bulbs, laid out like carpets, in their walled gardens. Cut tulips were wound around obelisks and archways, and massive vases were filled every day with fresh, full blooms. What the potentates preferred was the curvaceous, waisted kind of tulip that's known as "lily flowered" (though it has nothing to do with lilies and doesn't even particularly look like them), whose petals curve inwards at the centre, in the shape of a vase, and have pointy tips. Soon, stylized versions of this favourite new flower were cropping up on everything from their embroidered gold brocade robes to exquisite

ceramic wall tiles. The rulers also staged elaborate tulip festi-
vals at every new moon. They demanded that their guests show
up in exotic costumes that harmonized with the colours of
tulips—and perhaps even asked these party-goers to peel those
costumes off as the night wore on. For these were clearly lust-
fuelled affairs, featuring lots of belly dancing and squads of
nubile young ladies—likely members of the potentate's harem—
undulating without a stitch on around the candlelit vases.

In fact, the Turkish rulers got such a charge out of their
beloved tulips that they introduced severe punishments for
anyone—harem guard, dancing girl, party guest—caught swip-
ing their bulbs. Tyrannical and possessive to the core, they
undoubtedly wanted to keep the allure of these flowers a sexy
secret. Outside their gardens, no one was supposed to know
that tulips served as instruments of desire.

HANKY-PANKY BENEATH *the* CHANDELIERS

Count on the French. Once the tulip reached their shores, they
picked up where the tumescent Turks left off. Unlike their
neighbours in the Netherlands, the citizens of France never
speculated in tulips and—early in the seventeenth century at
least—they weren't particularly enamoured of planting the
bulbs in their gardens, either. Yet the Gallic well-to-do quickly

embraced the idea of using cut tulips as signals of availability—
or unavailability—in the romance department.

During the reign of the Sun King, Louis XIV, it became fash-
ionable for the ladies of the court to tuck a saucily positioned
tulip in their cleavage—preferably a very expensive one. And the
flower's colour said it all. In perhaps the first instance of the
fledgling language of flowers being used to convey a message,
the colour signified, to the horny males hovering around under
the crystal chandeliers at Versailles, whether the wearer was
ready, willing, and able to participate in a bit of hanky-panky.

A red tulip meant "declaration of passionate love" (in other
words, "Yes, I want you. Let's go"), yet a yellow tulip spelled
trouble because it denoted "hopeless love" ("I'd love to. I'm
mad about you, but alas I'm already taken by that big-nosed
jerk, standing over there in the purple pantaloons").

The Martha Stewarts of the day also spent small fortunes on
decorating their homes with bunches of cut tulips. These were
rushed to Paris by stagecoach from Haarlem (still the centre of
the Netherlands' bulb-growing empire) while they were still in
bud. Demand was so great, the Dutch actually worried that they
were going to run out of the flowers, and perhaps decided then
and there to go into the tulip business in a big way.

Later on, Empress Josephine also played a hand in spreading
tulips throughout Europe, due to her personal connection to a

Turkish sultan. The flower-mad wife of Napoleon had a beautiful, blue-eyed cousin from Martinique named Aimee de Rivery, who became a concubine in the court of Mahmud II at Constantinople, after a bizarre hijacking incident at sea. En route home to the Caribbean from a convent in Nantes, Aimee was ambushed by Algerians while sailing through the Mediterranean. She wound up being sold off to the Turks and, luckily for her, the potentate who bought her fell madly in love. When Aimee gave birth to a son in 1783, he was so overjoyed he held a gigantic tulip festival that shook the rafters of his palace. While it seems Josephine didn't personally attend this bash, she did exchange letters with her newly anointed Turkish relations, and more tulips undoubtedly got dispatched to the French capital as a consequence.

> The tulips should be behind
> bars like dangerous animals;
> They are opening like the mouth
> of some great African cat . . .
>
> SYLVIA PLATH, "TULIPS"

FLASHY PARROTS *provoke* PERKY IDEAS

For tulips that titillate, plant the parrots. Dismissed as too flashy for decades (hoity-horts who love pastel hues still turn up their noses at them), parrot tulips are favourites of floral designers. They've also seen a resurgence in popularity with hip young gardeners. It's about time, too.

Unlike traditional tulips, whose neat, cup-like shapes have a sculptural quality, parrots are gloriously messy confections. With their fringed, frilly petals, as exotic looking as a gypsy's shawl, they refuse to behave like good girls in the garden. On the contrary, these tulips love to flop all over the place, flaunting their charms as if in defiance of their upstanding cousins. And their colours can be as gaudy and delicious as the tropical birds they're named after. A few sexy specimens:

'Black Parrot': Glossy, frilly, and black, with fluted petals. Straight out of a Victoria's Secret catalogue.
'Estella Rijnveld': White streaked with rosy red. As yummy as raspberry ripple ice cream.
'Flaming Parrot': Chrome-yellow petals ignited with red. The leggiest parrot. Grows over 2 feet tall and thrashes around wildly on a windy day.
'Orange Favourite': A zinger combo of bright orange and pink, streaked with lime green.

for CERTAIN GENTLEMEN, *a* CONSUMING PASSION

Tulip bulbs taste similar to onions, but with a harder texture And indeed, during the Second World War, the starving Dutch raided tulip bulb fields to supplement their meagre rations. Yet

back when the first Elizabeth was on the throne, hardness of a different kind was anticipated from chowing on the underpinnings of these flowers. Tulip bulbs became the beluga caviar of the day for one simple reason: they were reputed to have a Viagra-like effect on those who ate them.

"I cannot say from my selfe, not having eaten many . . . if there are any special properties," wrote one gent cautiously to another, "but I think they may well have it."

A respected English botanist, John Parkinson, was skeptical about this claim. Yet he did recommend mashing tulip bulbs in red wine and then imbibing the disgusting concoction in order to cure "a cricke in the neck." And perhaps it had an effect in other areas of the anatomy too.

The Virgin Queen, meanwhile, used the flowers to turn off males intent on courting her. She reportedly had white tulip designs—the symbol of innocence—embroidered on her gowns

as a subtle signal to potential suitors that they had better not
entertain any ideas about entering her bedchamber.

Love Potion Number 15

Candied tulip petals, sold in Japanese supermarkets, make
a novel prelude to love. To candy your own, use pink or red
tulips that have come up for the second time in your
garden (the bulbs will no longer carry any traces of
pesticides). Pick flower heads early in the morning and pull
petals off carefully, so they aren't bruised. Dip petals in
lightly beaten egg white and shake off any excess. Lay them
on a cookie sheet spread with a layer of fine sugar, then
turn the petals over and dip in sugar again. Leave to dry on
a rack. Use up quickly.

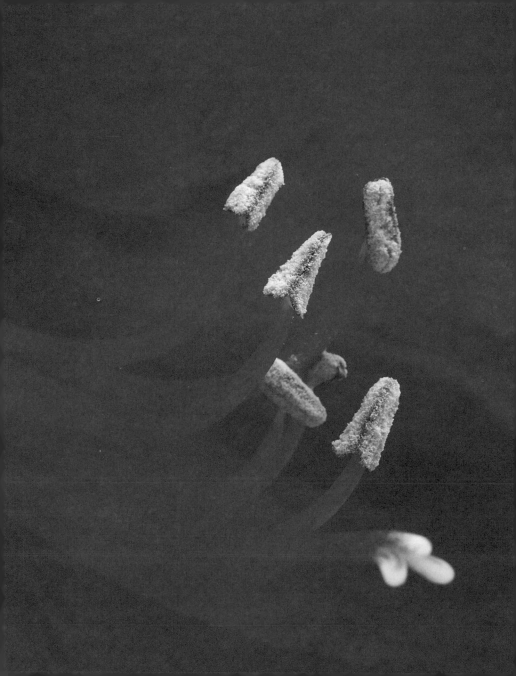

RAPTURE

THE AMARYLLIS
The beauty with the hot-to-trot stalk

Ah, the amaryllis. So cocky. So lusty. So full of life. It's no surprise that millions of women all over the world adore this easy-to-grow tropical houseplant.

Just ask any garden centre, florist, or mail-order bulb supplier that sells amaryllis bulbs. The answer will probably be the same everywhere you go, from downtown Manhattan to Melbourne, Australia. When it comes to buyers, females outnumber males—often by as much as two to one.

"Ladies love amaryllis, especially when they're already potted up and starting to grow," confirms the owner of an upscale flower shop in the East Seventies of New York. "I just have to put the pots in the window in October and women start coming in. But . . ." he adds, with a mischievous chuckle, "my gay customers love them too. I think it has something to do with the stalk."

Yes, that stalk—known as a "scape." Fat and rounded, with a slightly bulbous bit at the tip, the scape is where the flower head sits, gradually thickening up as it prepares to burst into the world. And it flirts with us, no question. To look at a long pale green scape is to want to reach out and stroke it. Lovingly, from top to bottom. (Resist the urge, though. Touching will leave unsightly fingermarks, because the surface of the scape is covered in a fine powder.)

Who hasn't felt mildly titillated by the sight of a scape strutting on a window ledge, during a dreary January day? This plant is the perfect antidote to the flatness of winter—jaunty, optimistic, life-affirming and always so eager to get down to the business of satisfying our desire for its spectacular blooms. Indeed, watching a scape's meteoric march upwards is a reminder to anyone who lives in a northern climate that spring will eventually show its face again. There may be grim-looking slush and bare branches beyond the window right now, yet soon everything will turn green and fertile once more, and plants will start

popping up in our gardens with wonderful abandon—just like
that saucy scape.

JET PROPELLED—*with* A PURPOSE

It's fascinating to watch the scape on an amaryllis grow. With
some varieties, you can almost observe this happening—the
scape will lengthen, as if by magic, several inches
every day. This protuberance serves a practical
purpose: hollow, sturdy, and leafless, it's strong
enough to support an enormous bloom and also
stores water to keep the plant alive.

In fact, there is so much water in an amaryllis
stalk, keep a cloth handy when you're cutting it
down after the blooms are done. A disconcerting
amount of liquid can gush out of this hose-like apparatus—and
who wants to put a damper on a wonderful love affair by wreck-
ing the coffee table?

FLESHY FOLDS *like* SILKY LINGERIE

The scape's rocket-like progress is irresistible fun to watch. But
stick around for what happens next, when the covering of its
bulbous tip peels back. This covering, known as the "spathe,"

starts out a leafy green, but dries out and splits open when the plant is ready to release the flower heads. Then this wisp shrivels away into nothingness—often in the space of a day—and it's time for the real show. Long, drooping petals—hitherto jampacked together, layer upon layer, as if in a space capsule—start unfurling. And how wickedly sexy they look, these seductive, fleshy folds, almost like some silky slip dropped on to a sofa during an amorous encounter. Or, equally titillating, the sexual organs of a woman. Backlit by shafts of winter sun coming through the window, the petals glow, shimmer, and turn transparent in the light, and—in some varieties—they have a remarkable resemblance to human skin, because a spiderwork of little veins is detectable, running through each petal.

Touching is permitted now. Stroke the petals. Feel the sensuous texture under your fingertips, although, careful . . . Don't tweak the long golden stamens and even longer pistil that poke out provocatively from the tight little crevice at the centre of the flower. Golden grains of pollen piled on the stamen ends will come off and stain everything with a vivid yellow that is impossible to remove from clothing. Stand back and observe as each flower package, truly a miracle of design, opens up over a day or two into a mammoth flower head. (Amaryllis blooms have the distinction of being among the largest in the world.) Marvel at this radiant gift from Mother Nature—so stimulating to the senses on a cold winter's day—and at how she manages to pull the feat off with virtually no help from us.

And then wonder why gardening books and catalogues persist in describing the amaryllis in bland and uninspiring terms like "striking," "popular," and "very special." This taken-for-granted houseplant deserves better. Unquestionably erotic, yet in a delightful, unassuming way, it's a botanical wonder too.

AMARYLLIS *as* DRACULA'S BRIDE?

Talk about blood and guts. The story of this popular plant could be made into a horror movie. According to classical myths, Amaryllis was a sweet young thing who fell madly in love with a cold-hearted cad called Alteo. He was a shepherd—one of those dark, curly-haired Greek-god types who habitually make women's hearts go pitter-pat. But Alteo seems to have been a plant geek too, because he spurned Amaryllis, saying that his only desire was to see a new flower, one that had never existed in the world before.

Devastated, she consulted the oracle at Delphi and received some painful advice: "Pierce your heart with a golden arrow, dearie, right outside Alteo's door." Ouch. Yet Amaryllis, completely smitten with Alteo, obeyed. Then the nubile nymph kept

showing up on his doorstep for thirty consecutive nights, dripping blood all over her white maiden's robes. Looking like a
bride of Dracula, perhaps. At any rate, Alteo refused to pay
attention (he was a plant geek, remember). So when he finally
did open the door, a flower with scarlet petals had started growing there, sprung from the blood of by-now-dead Amaryllis.

Not a pretty tale, but as a consequence, "Amaryllis" became
the standard moniker given to a shepherdess in classical poetry.
Ovid wrote about her. So did the British poet John Milton who
expressed an ardent desire to "sport with Amaryllis in the shade."
This flower has, in fact, remained resolutely female throughout
history. She now symbolizes a range of qualities—splendid
beauty, haughty loveliness, feminine pride—which are appropriate, given her spectacular trumpet-shaped blooms, poised
atop those long stalks. Yet at the same time, surely the most lov-
able quality of the amaryllis is that she is such an accessible
plant—not at all disdainful, in fact—because anyone can plant a
bulb in a pot and be assured that it will produce glorious flowers
with absolutely no effort at all.

The modern Greek words *amarysso* and *amarussein* mean
"to sparkle, twinkle, scintillate, or shine," and they seem to fit
this tropical beauty far better. The amaryllis does indeed sparkle
in our homes in winter—elegant, eye-catching, with a frisson
of excitement thrown in to make us smile.

AMOROUS AMARYLLIS

Fire-engine red is traditional, but try these varieties for a change. They all look particularly luscious when their petals start unfurling.

'Aphrodite': Named after the goddess of love. Pink and white curly petals, edged with pink. Enormous blooms.

'Black Pearl': Misleading name. In reality, the deep, delectable red of Victorian boudoirs. Erotic quotient high, because the stamens and pistil are a vivid scarlet.

'Dancing Queen': A leggy Carmen, with masses of gypsy skirts in tangerine mixed with white.

'Lady Jane': Pinkish flowers, medium-sized. Lots of petal layers. A Victorian miss in her underwear.

'Naughty Lady': Tall. Saucy, pinkish, medium-sized flowers striped in white.

'Nymph': A mini, at half the height of her sisters. Virginal white flowers streaked in a teasing pinkish-orange.

'Sweet Surrender': Fairly tall. Huge white flowers bordered in pink, with subtle highlights throughout the petals.

of ROMAN EMPERORS *and* NAUGHTY LADIES

Tropical bulbs that we call "amaryllis" come from a huge and complicated family of plants known as *Amaryllidaceae*. In fact, strictly speaking, they're not really amaryllis at all, but *Hippeastrum*. The plant pooh-bahs came up with this cumbersome and unattractive definition a while ago (it means "horse star") but the word doesn't fit the flowers at all. Now only hoity-horts who want to sound posh use the term. (Don't go into a garden centre asking to see their hippeastrums. The staff will likely look blank and wonder what the heck you're talking about.) Within this widespread family, there's a whole slew of seductive charmers. Two that have aroused passions in the past:

Jersey lily *Amaryllis belladonna*: Not a true lily, this is a beautiful imposter with a naughty history. Originally from South Africa, the bulb produces spidery pink flowers (also sometimes white streaked with pink or violet) that can be grown out of doors in the southern United States. Its name is inspired by Lily Langtry, the commoner who became the infamous mistress of King Edward VII. Born in Jersey, one of the Channel Islands off France, she socialized with the likes of Oscar Wilde and James McNeill Whistler, scandalizing the British upper crust at the turn of the twentieth century. The plant got dubbed "Jersey lily" because a British painter, John Everett Millais, did a famous and lovely painting of Langtry holding what is purportedly a "Jersey lily." Confusingly, though, what's really in her hands is a scarlet Guernsey lily, *Nerine samiensis*, which is the national flower of Jersey's neighbouring island.

Love Potion Number 16

JERSEY LILY COCKTAIL

Did Lily Langtry serve this to her royal lover before a torrid tumble at their London love nest? Probably not. King Edward VII was a pot-bellied old goat with a penchant for the hard stuff. However, the cocktail that bears her name is popular today with teetotallers as it's refreshing yet non-alcoholic.

1   wine glass sparkling apple juice

2   dashes of Angostura bitters

¼   teaspoon sugar

Shake the ingredients well with ice. Strain into a wine glass. Decorate with a cocktail cherry.

Naked lily *Lycoris squamigera*: Sounds like a ghastly skin disease
or masticated candy, but far from it. This is a lissome, leggy
charmer with big, sea-shell pink flowers. She gets her
name from a Roman actress called
Lycoris, who was the mistress of
Mark Antony (presumably before
Cleopatra, his last love). She grows
in the same way as a regular potted
amaryllis but can be planted out
of doors in warmer areas of North
America to bloom in August. Her
other nicknames include surprise
lily, magic lily, and resurrection
lily—because the big flowers with
long, elegant stamens always appear
first. Then green strappy leaves
that are characteristic of classic
amaryllis pop up and stick around, brightening the garden
all winter.

However, *Lycoris* doesn't have a romantic image to everyone. The Chinese call this flower *Zhongkui*, after a fierce-
looking ghost warrior who fights demons.

DEVOTION

THE COCO DE MER
The salacious siren and her loyal lover

Positively pornographic. That's the coco de mer. In fact, if you're the kind of person who hates hearing graphic details, don't bother reading on—because this truly extraordinary fruit and its reputed reproductive habits are a shocker. Everyone who encounters this "coconut" for the first time is immediately struck by how sexually explicit it looks. Embarrassingly so. Even grown men have been known to blush, chuckle, and make comments like "Whew," "Unbelievable," and "What a hottie."

Why? Just look. And be amazed—because the "lady fruit" (to use one of her more printable nicknames) resembles almost exactly the pelvic region of a naked human female—in size, shape, weight, virtually everything. She's even equipped with a Mount of Venus and a few wisps of pubic "hair." Then turn her over, and the erotic quotient notches even higher. A round, perfectly formed butt stares back at you—its cheeks spread invitingly wide, with an impossible-to-ignore crack situated between the two.

That's not all, either. Consider the way this curvaceous creature is said to go about producing little coco de mers. She apparently seeks the services of a male counterpart sporting a phallic tool that's as thick and long as a man's arm. This flagrant appendage points stiffly upwards, like a monstrous erection, and is said to sidle up devotedly to his lady love at the full moon. Then they mate. Noisily and with much thrashing about. Yet humans are advised not to witness the frenzied coupling, because if they do, they'll be instantly turned into black parrots.

Endowed with such a carnal *curriculum vitae*, the coco de mer can certainly lay claim to being the most erotically charged plant on the planet. Human males who've encountered her would undoubtedly agree—and many have had the pleasure.

She has tormented sex-starved sailors who fished her out of the sea. She made Malaysian and Indian rulers so crazy to possess her, they forked over fortunes. Way back in the eighteenth century, one of her admirers, King Gustavus of Sweden, spent four thousand gold florins to acquire her and then showed off her eye-popping prurience in his curiosity cabinet. The French painter Gauguin was so captivated, he did a sculpture of her backside. And nowadays, Coco de Mer is the name of an upscale sex shop in Covent Garden, London.

This flagrant fruit is imbued with so much sexuality, no other plant comes close. Not even the most blatant of orchids. So here she is, deliciously exposed in all her lewd loveliness, as a fitting climax to these spicy tales of love and lust in the plant world.

HOW CAN *you* GET YOUR HANDS *on* A COCO DE MER?

In short, down, boy. You can't. But first, the boring botanical bits. Strictly speaking, despite her name, she's not a coconut at all, but the seed of a kind of palm tree called *Lodoicea maldivica*, which belongs to the *Arecaceae* family. And this object bears the distinction of being the largest and heaviest seed in the world, weighing in at 50 pounds or more. It develops on the female version of the *Lodoicea* palm, which can soar over 100 feet into the sky. Yet before these seeds start appearing, get a load of her flowers. They're pretty titillating too. They look, it has to be said, rather like women's breasts, right down to their centre ovules, which resemble moist nipples—and they ooze nectar. Coco's "suitor," meanwhile, the male *Lodoicea*, sends forth its fat, tube-shaped protuberance called a catkin, which extends to a couple of feet and is covered in sweet-smelling yellow flowers shaped like stars. After pollination (in reality by insects and bats, who carry pollen from the male flowers to the female ones), this eye-popping tumescence shrivels and sags, eventually falling off the tree, while the fertilized seed keeps on swelling to her enormous, suggestive shape.

Love Potion Number 17

Take a coco de mer, about a year old, which shows a thin gold band near the crown. It's now at its peak of edibility. Slice the fruit open and eat the custard-like flesh before making love. It is a powerful aphrodisiac, especially for men.

OLD BELIEF

She's in no hurry, though. Like another tease of the plant kingdom, the seed of the vanilla orchid, Coco refuses to be rushed. Seven long years—that's how long the progeny of this palm requires to reach maturity. It's one reason why we can't get our hands on her. She's in short supply. The other problem is that this sexually charged oddity is as elusive as Greta Garbo was. She grows well in only one place on the planet, and they've introduced stiff conservation laws there, due to her diminishing numbers. If you visit and try to steal a coco de mer, you might wind up languishing with the cockroaches and rats in a cramped, sweaty tropical jail. For a long, long time.

That's because her homeland is the Seychelles. Located between East Africa and India, and north of Madagascar, they're a ribbon of tiny, palm-fringed islands, popular with tourists for their idyllic beaches, yet so microscopic on world maps it's easy to miss them completely. Adding to her allure is the fact that two—only two of these drops in the big blue bucket of the Indian Ocean are graced by coco de mer's arousing presence. The islands in question are called Praslin and Curieuse. For reasons that have baffled botanists, the "nut" that's shaped like a human butt stubbornly refuses to put down roots anywhere else.

LOVE OBJECT *of* A FAMOUS BRITISH GENERAL

Comely coco de mer has always inspired fantasies of the ooh-la-la kind. But hundreds of years ago, she was also regarded as a sort of watery goddess, living in the sea. Hence her name. People believed that she sprang from the ocean floor, sending up long, swaying fronds to the surface, because sailors would find the giant seeds floating on the currents and excitedly haul them back to land, yet no one could figure out where they came from. Just about everyone—Arab traders, Indian and Asian rulers, European explorers, French botanists, rogue privateers of all nationalities—believed this myth. Some even swore they spotted the fronds moving sensually to and fro, under the waves. Because they looked so erotic, the seeds became endowed with magical powers and were sought after as fertility symbols. Arab potentates wanted them for their harems. Indian religious sects placed the nuts on altars and worshipped them. Canny sailors made fortunes by flogging prize specimens they found to eager buyers around the world. And anyone who stole a coco de mer from an important pooh-bah didn't go to jail as poachers do now. He had his hands cut off. It wasn't until 1756 that the mystery of her origins was solved. European cartographers mapping the Indian Ocean sailed into the Seychelles—hitherto so tucked away, they were unknown—and discovered *Lodoicea* palms growing in thousands on Praslin island.

The coco de mer is a miracle of nature and, of all things living in the sea, the most rare.

EAST INDIAN LEGEND

End of story? Not quite. Even with her birthplace revealed, Coco continued to confound every visitor who encountered her, due to her startling appearance. Take General Charles Gordon. This stiff-upper-lip Brit, famous veteran of countless battles on behalf of Queen Victoria's burgeoning colonial empire, visited the Seychelles in 1885 and promptly fell in love with its tropical lushness. He became convinced he'd arrived in the true Garden of Eden. To him, the sexy coco de mer was the tree of knowledge. No doubt about that, he insisted. He drew detailed diagrams of her, trying to prove his point. But Gordon died shortly afterwards in a celebrated battle at Khartoum, and his engaging theory about the Edenic origins of man, inspired by the most libidinous living thing ever to appear in the plant kingdom, never got taken seriously.

the REAL FORBIDDEN FRUIT

Whither the comely coco de mer? That's debatable today. She's certainly struggling a bit. There are only about 24,000 of these palms left. Two-thirds won't be able to bear those fabled "nuts" for years, and half of the trees are males, anyway. Yet poachers are still sneaking in and plundering places where they grow because wealthy anonymous clients are willing to fork over fist-fuls of dough just to get their hands on this incredible botanical

phenomenon. And as our crowded world closes in on the no-longer-isolated Seychelles, the coco de mer has, inevitably, become a hot tourist attraction.

Outside Praslin airport, where jam-packed jets arrive in a steady stream from Europe, there's now a gigantic sculpture of the nut, surrounded by four fountains shaped like the phallic male *Lodoicea* flowers. These spray her flanks regularly, making them glisten in the tropical sun—an explicit demonstration of ardour that prompts titters from passing tourists as they head in taxis up to the Vallée de Mai forest reserve to ogle over Coco in her natural habitat. In this windy setting, where the slim, sky-scraper palm reaches upwards into humid tropical clouds and waves noisily back and forth, flinging her messy detritus of fronds, expired protuberances, and other bits and pieces down to the forest floor, she's now watched over by eagle-eyed Seychellois forest rangers. And what's immediately apparent, when you meet them, is that the coco de mer has truly become the forbidden fruit, Garden of Eden or not. "No picking up of anything in the reserve," decree these young, zealous, khaki-uniformed protectors. "And no tasting of a fruit you find on the ground either." Yes, ma'am. We'll do nothing but look, promise.

HOW *to* MAKE LOVE LAST

What keeps a spouse as faithful and snuggly as coco de mer's loyal love? For centuries, wives have enlisted the aid of plants to tame hubby's roving eye. A few examples:

Crocus: Long regarded as a potent aid to arousal. Cleopatra made an ointment from the oil of crocus and rubbed it into her palms before letting her hands wander all over Mark Antony. And in a Greek legend, Homer was said to have spread a mat of crocus flowers in the spot where the King and Queen of Heaven lay together.

Love Potion Number 18

Take a quantity of dried rose and violet petals, plus some saffron, myrrh, lavender, and rosemary. Mix with an equal amount of the dried flesh of a viper, and steep in honey. Mix into wine. OLD ROMAN APHRODISIAC

Dragon tree *Dracaena draco*: If hubby stayed out too late in the Solomon Islands, lonely wives burned a strong-smelling incense made from this tree to bring him back. It produces cherry-sized fruits that exude a thick scarlet resin said to resemble the blood of dragons. Abandoned women dried the stuff into chunks, then burned it next to an open window for seven consecutive nights. If they stopped this ritual before the prescribed time, their men would never return.

Mimosa *Acacia dealbata*: Adored by Italians (its fuzzy yellow powder puffs of flowers often peep enticingly over crumbling walls in Venice), mimosa is also instantly recognizable in wedding bouquets all over the world. And although this shrub is actually native to Australia, the flowers function as a symbol of faithfulness in many cultures. Suspending a sprig of mimosa above the marriage bed will, one Arab legend goes, lengthen love and ward off jealousy.

Myrtle *Lagerstroemia indica*: Symbol of lasting love in ancient
Greece. Still popular in Europe. Victorian brides put myrtle
in their wedding bouquets. So did Princess Anne, when she
married Mark Phillips in 1973, although its effectiveness was
clearly a bit iffy. (They divorced.) Anne's cutting originated
with Queen Victoria's own wedding sprig of myrtle, taken
from a bush planted at Osborne House, in the Isle of Wight,
after her nuptials with Albert. Thus, Kate Middleton got the
secateurs out again before she walked down the aisle with
her William in April 2011. (Let's hope Waitie Katie has better
luck than her horsy aunt-in-law.)

Sweet mignonette *Reseda phyteuma*: Cottage garden plant with a
musky scent that's said to mimic female sex pheromones.
Botanists like Pliny the Elder and Linnaeus thought so and
described it as an aphrodisiac. One big fan was Napoleon.
He reportedly preferred his missus, Josephine, not to wash
before their amorous encounters, but clearly he wasn't
opposed to *un petit peu de parfum floral*—he dispatched seeds
of sweet mignonette home to her while fighting battles in
Egypt. British poet William Cowper subsequently dubbed
the plant "Frenchman's darling."

Rosemary *Rosmarinus*: Mediterranean herb with spiky, resinous
leaves. Probably the most potent symbol of fidelity ever. Used
by everyone from the Romans (who entwined it in bridal

bouquets) to horrid old Henry VIII (he of the six wives, two of whom got the chop for adultery). In the Song of Solomon, the bride is counselled to put three rosemary leaves between the pages of a Bible. Then, to receive lasting love from her man, she must place the holy book under his pillow.

Love Potion Number 19

ROSEMARY BRIDAL DRINK

- 2 cups lime juice
- 2 tablespoons chopped rosemary leaves, wrapped in cheesecloth
- 2 cups sliced strawberries
- 6 cups ginger ale (or ginger wine)

Sugar and water to taste

Mix all ingredients together in a punch bowl. Remove rosemary 20 minutes later, or the flavour will be too strong. Serve over ice.

During Henry's reign, rosemary ruled at wedding rites. Newly married couples dipped sprigs in their cups of wine, a tradition that still persists in Italy. More of the herb was strewn in their bed linen. The bride was also advised to present her groom with yet another sprig before they hopped between the sheets. And the man in question needed to pretend, if necessary, to like the powerful smell (even though many males hate it) because if he objected, people believed he would be lousy in bed.

Empress Josephine, meanwhile, reached for the herb at bath time. Although Napoleon liked her to come to bed *au naturel,* she expected him to take a bath in rosemary water first. Rinsing his mouth out with this scented liquid was also a requirement.

Napoleon's missus genuinely loved rosemary. She grew lots at Malmaison, their house outside Paris, a place she adored and where she continued to live after he abandoned her. Her passion for this herb certainly fits. There's another old belief that aromatic rosemary will flourish only in a house where the woman rules.

The flower is the poetry of reproduction. It is an example of the eternal seductiveness of life.

JEAN GIRAUDOUX

Author's Acknowledgements

Some books spring from lofty ideas, but this one had its beginnings with a remarkably sexy butternut squash. Her luscious "buttocks" were spotted by a gardening buddy, Sara Katz, in an alleyway in downtown Toronto, where the squash had somehow managed to insinuate itself into a backyard fence. Sara said I simply had to write about it in my *Toronto Star* gardening column. When my agent, Carolyn Forde, read the column and saw the accompanying photo by Barrie Murdock (visit www.soniaday.com to see the photo), she said, as agents are wont to do, "I think there's a book in this." Thus, *The Untamed Garden* was born.

Yet all books, irrespective of where the idea originated, are a team effort, involving many enthusiastic individuals. I particularly want to thank Anita Chong, senior editor at McClelland & Stewart, who immediately liked the idea of a book about erotic plants and flowers, and who used her imagination to come up with an entertaining format. She also contributed many valuable suggestions about the style and content of the chapters.

My grateful thanks also go to:

Senior designer Terri Nimmo, who spent countless hours on the project and included me every step of the way.

M&S president and publisher, Doug Pepper, who trusted Anita's hunch that the idea was sound and could be turned into a readable book.

Researcher Mary Fran McQuade, who dug up a wealth of fascinating tidbits about plant folklore.

Copy editor and punctuation pro Wendy Dennis, who spotted some important errors in my historical accounts of plants.

The sales, marketing, and publicity team at M&S, especially publicity manager Ashley Dunn, and all the individuals in bookstores, online, and elsewhere, who work tirelessly to help authors like me find an audience.

The botanical artists and photographers both past and present, including my partner, Barrie Murdock, whose images have made this book come alive.

Sean Sinclair Day, for his valiant efforts to come up with a title that satisfied everyone.

Cactus aficionados Mary McLenahan and Jim Peck of Oaxaca, Mexico, who set me straight on the complexities of the amazing cereus.

Mystery writer Michelle Wan and Tom Atkinson of the Southern Ontario Orchid Society (www.soos.ca), who expanded my knowledge of orchids.

The lovely ladies (and one gent) who volunteer their services at the Toronto Botanical Garden's Weston Family Library, and the equally helpful librarians at the Fergus Branch of the Wellington County Library. Thanks to them all, I didn't stop uncovering amazing stuff about plants for months.

All the web sites, bloggers, and contributors to the internet (too many to mention individually) who provided food for thought.

All my gardening buddies who contributed valuable suggestions and kept asking, "How's the book going?"

Finally, my lovely agent, Carolyn Forde of Westwood Creative Artists, for coming up with the idea and encouraging me to write this book.

Bibliography

Bristow, Alec. *The Sex Life of Plants: A Study of the Secrets of Reproduction*. New York: Holt, Rinehart, and Winston, 1978.

Gollner, Adam Leith. *The Fruit Hunters: A Story of Nature, Adventure, Commerce and Obsession*. Toronto: Anchor Canada, 2008.

Hansen, Eric. *Orchid Fever: A Horticultural Tale of Love, Lust, and Lunacy*. New York: Pantheon Books, 2000.

Loewer, Peter. *The Evening Garden: Flowers and Fragrance from Dusk Till Dawn*. New York: MacMillan Publishing Co., 1993.

Sanders, Dawn. "Carnivorous Plants: Science and the Literary Imagination." *Planta Carnivora* 32, 1 (Spring 2010): 30–34.

Further Reading

Ackerman, Diane. *Cultivating Delight*. New York: HarperCollins, 2001.

Albertson, Michael and Ellen. *Temptations: Igniting the Pleasure and Power of Aphrodisiacs*. New York: Simon & Schuster, 2002.

Bales, Suzanne. *A Garden of Fragrance*. Toronto: HarperCollins, 2000.

Barnstone, Tony, and Ping Chou. *Chinese Erotic Poems*. Toronto: Random House of Canada, 2007.

Boland, Bridget. *Gardener's Magic and Other Old Wives' Lore*. London: Michael O'Mara, 2003.

Branning, Katharine. *Yes, I Would Like Another Glass of Tea: An American Woman's Letters to Turkey*. New York: Blue Dome Press, 2010.

Carr, David McClain. *The Erotic Word: Sexuality, Spirituality and the Bible*. New York: Oxford University Press, 2003.

Cerwinske, Laura. *The Book of the Rose*. London: Thames and Hudson, 1992.

Day, Sonia. *Tulips: Facts and Folklore About the World's Most Planted Flower.* Toronto: Key Porter Books, 2001.

de Luca, Diane. *Botanica Erotica: Arousing Body, Mind and Spirit.* Vermont: Healing Arts Press, 1978.

Detienne, Marcel. *The Gardens of Adonis: Spices in Greek Mythology.* Princeton, New Jersey: Princeton University Press, 1977.

Emboden, William. *Bizarre Plants.* New York: Macmillan, 1974.

Hamill, Sam (ed.). *The Erotic Spirit: An Anthology of Poems of Sensuality, Love and Longing.* Boston and London: Shambhala Publications, 1999.

Harding, Alice. *The Peony.* Portland, Oregon: Timber Press, 1993.

Heiser, Charles B., Jr. *The Fascinating World of the Nightshades.* New York: Dover Publications, 1969.

Hewitt, Terry. *The Complete Book of Cacti and Succulents.* London: Dorling Kindersley, 1993.

Hughes, Holly. *Gardens: Quotations on the Perennial Pleasures of Soil, Seed and Sun.* Philadelphia: Running Press, 1994.

Lerner, Ernst and Johanna. *Folklore and Symbolism of Flowers, Plants and Trees.* New York: Tudor Publishing, 1960.

Loewer, Peter. *Jefferson's Garden.* Mechanicsburg, Pennsylvania: Stackpole Books, 2004.

Mace, Tony and Suzanne. *Cactus and Succulents.* San Diego: Laurel Glen Publishing, 1998.

Overy, Angela. *Sex in Your Garden.* Colorado: Fulcrum Publishing, 1997.

Powell, Claire. *The Meaning of Flowers.* London: Jupiter Books, 1977.

Simonds, Merilyn. *Gardens: A Literary Companion.* Vancouver: Greystone Books, 2008.

Valder, Peter. *Garden Plants of China.* Portland, Oregon: Timber Press, 1999.

Vickery, Roy. *Oxford Dictionary of Plant-Lore.* Oxford: Oxford University Press, 1997.

Wan, Michelle. *Deadly Slipper: A Novel of Death in the Dordogne.* New York: Vintage Books, 2006.

Text Acknowledgements

27. Excerpt from untitled peony poem by Angela Leuck, as published in her blog entry, "Passion for Peonies." A Poet in the Garden. July 17, 2009. www. acleuck.blogspot.com. Reprinted by permission of the author.

31. Excerpt from "Girl" by Eve Alexandra, from *The Drowned Girl* by Eve Alexandra. Kent: Kent State University Press (2003).

46. "Weaving a Garland Long Ago" by Anakreon, ca. 570 BC, from *The Erotic Spirit: An Anthology of Poems of Sensuality, Love, and Longing,* edited by Sam Hamill. Boston: Shambhala Publications, Inc. (1996). www.shambhala.com.

55. "See How the Roses Burn!" by Hafiz, translated by Ralph Waldo Emerson.

63. Excerpt from "The force that through the green fuse drives the flower" by Dylan Thomas, from *The Collected Poems of Dylan Thomas.* New York: New Directions Publishing Corp. (2010).

82. Excerpt from "The Spring Flowers Own" by Etel Adnan, from *The Spring Flowers Own & The Manifestations of the Voyage* by Etel Adnan. Sausalito: The Post Apollo Press (1990).

110. Excerpt from *A Natural History of the Senses* by Diane Ackerman. New York: Vintage Books (1995).

125. Excerpt from "Peas" by Lorna Crozier, from *The Blue Hour of the Day: Selected Poems by Lorna Crozier.* Toronto: McClelland & Stewart (2007).

139. Excerpt from "To the Tune of 'A floating cloud crosses enchanted mountain'" by Huang E, translated by Kenneth Rexroth, from *The Orchid Boat: Women Poets of China* by Kenneth Rexroth. New York: McGraw-Hill (1972). As published in *Chinese Erotic Poems,* edited by Tony Barnstone and Chou Ping. New York: Alfred A. Knopf (Everyman's Library edition) (2007).

179. Excerpt from "Tulips" by Sylvia Plath, from *The Collected Poems* by Sylvia Plath. New York: HarperCollins (2008).

i. Portrait of frangipani and marigolds native to Mexico. © National Geographic Society / CORBIS. ii. Fruit, 1897. Lithograph, 66 x 44 cm. Alphonse Mucha (1860–1939). © Banque d'Images, ADAGP / Art Resource, NY. v. Forget-me-not courtesy of Calibas at en.wikipedia. vi. *Two Calla Lilies on Pink*, 1928. Georgia O'Keeffe (1887–1986). © The Philadelphia Museum of Art / Art Resource, NY. viii. Red tulips, close up, white background © JAPACK / amanaimagesRF / amanaimages / CORBIS. 6. *Le Lys blanc: Lilium candidum* (detail). Pierre Joseph Redouté (1759–1840). Reproduced by permission of RHS, Lindley Library. 8. *Annunciation* (detail; full painting on facing page). Leonardo da Vinci (1472–1475). Oil and tempera on wood. Galleria degli Uffizi, Florence, Italy. 20. Detail of colourful peony taken at the Botanical gardens in NYC © Christine Michaud / GetStock.com. 23. Pink peony © Barrie Murdock. 26. Crimson peony, *Paeonia officinalis* © Florilegius / GetStock.com. 32. *Paeonia viewing* (Japanese garden prints). Coloured woodcut. Hiroshige II Utagawa (1826–1869). © The LuEsther T. Mertz Library, NYBG / Art Resource, NY. 37. Red anthurium © Tamara_k / Dreamstime.com. 38. "No Rest for the Wicked," 1935. © Illustrated London News Ltd. / Mary Evans Picture Library. 40. Gloire de Dijon Rosier Ile – Bourbon. Royal Botanic Gardens, Kew. Copyright © RBG KEW. 44. Illustrated colour plate from seed catalog for roses © Cynthia Hart Designer / CORBIS. 48. Rose petals © Photor455 / Dreamstime.com. 60. USA – Corpse Flower Blooms © Ted Soqui / CORBIS. 64. *Amorphophallus Titanum*. Matilda Smith (1854–1926). *Curtis's Botanical Magazine*, v. 117, ser. 3; v. 47 (1891) Image provided by Missouri Botanical Garden Library, www.mobot.org. 68. Jack-in-the-Pulpit © Amber Estabrooks / Dreamstime.com. 73. Monster Cactus at the Royal Botanic Gardens, Kew, 1845. © Illustrated London News Ltd. / Mary Evans Picture Library. 76. Tropical flora dark background © Joanne Zh / Dreamstime.com. 80. The trap of a Venus flytrap, showing trigger hairs. Photograph courtesy Noah Elhardt, via Wikimedia Commons. 86. Pitcher plant © Barrie Murdock. 88. Illustration of a

Variety of Insect-Eating Plants © Bettmann / CORBIS. **92:** *Epiphyllum oxypetalum* (night-blooming cereus, 'Queen of the Night') © Joseph Dougherty, MD / ecology.org. **99.** Illustration of *Cereus triangularis Blanco*. In *Flora de Filipinas* [...] Gran edición [...] Tomo Cuarto, 1880–1883, by Francisco Manuel Blanco (O.S.A.). **100.** *Cereus hexagonus* (L.) Mill. © Joseph Dougherty, MD / ecology.org. **112:** *Figs*, 1995 (w/c on paper) by Margaret Ann Eden (Contemporary Artist). Private Collection / The Bridgeman Art Library. **120.** *Proserpine*, 1882 (oil on canvas) by Dante Charles Gabriel Rossetti (1828–1882). Private Collection / Photo © Christie's Images / The Bridgeman Art Library. **123.** Tomato © Barrie Murdock. **126.** Litchis (Lychees) *euphoria litchi*, ca. 1845. © Mary Evans Picture Library. **128.** *The Garden of Earthly Delights* (detail: central panel inside, left side). Hieronymus Bosch (c. 1450–1516). Museo Nacional del Prado, Madrid, Spain. **130.** White orchid © Barrie Murdock. **132.** *Masdevallia roezlii*. John Day (1824–1888). In *The John Day Scrapbooks*, vol. 42, page 47. HLAA–(Herbarium, Library, Art). Royal Botanic Gardens, Kew. Copyright © RBG-KEW. **138.** *Cypripedium calceolus*. Anton Hartinger (1806–1890), via Wikimedia Commons. Illustration 448, vol. 4 in *Atlas der Alpenflora* (1882). **148.** *The Orchid*, 1899. A print from *The Magazine of Art*, Cassell and Company, Limited, 1899. © The Print Collector / Heritage-Images / Imagestate. **150.** Red orchid © Barrie Murdock. **152.** *Mandragore* [Mandragora mas]. From John Sibthorp, *Flora Graeca*, London, 1806, plate 76. © The LuEsther T. Mertz Library, NYBG / Art Resource, NY. **157.** *Atropa Mandragora*, ca. 1806–ca. 1840. Detailed study of plant with its flowers, root and seeds. James Sowerby (1757–1822). Plate 232 from *Flora Graeca*, (vol. 1-7) elaboravit J. E. Smith. (vol. 8-10 J. Lindley.) L.P., by John Sibthorp. (London, 1806–1840). © The British Library / Heritage-Images / Imagestate. **160.** Dioscorides/Mandrake, ca. 80 AD. © Mary Evans Picture Library. **166.** *Adam*, 1528 (oil on panel) by Lucas Cranach, the Elder (1472–1553). Galleria degli Uffizi, Florence, Italy / The Bridgeman Art Library. **170.** Tulip © Barrie Murdock. **174.** Red tulip, named 'Flame of Love' © Barrie Murdock. **176.** Tulip © Barrie Murdock. **180.** Watercolour on paper of Tulipa. August Wilhelm Sievert (–1751). Plate 12 in *Hortus florum imaginum* (ca. 1730). Reproduced by permission of RHS, Lindley Library. **182.** Bulb of tulip

© Ronalds Stikans / Dreamstime.com. **184.** Amaryllis flower close-up © Jose Luis Gutierrez / Vetta / Getty Images. **186:** Amaryllis scape © Barrie Murdock. **187.** Amaryllis flower © Mike Rogal / Dreamstime.com. **188.** Amaryllis © Tyson Erb. **190.** *Amaryllis.* Jan Bertus Heukelom (1875–1965). In *Dekorative Vorbilder: eine Sammlung von figürlichen Darstellungen und kunstgewerblichen Verzierungen.* © Picture Collection. The New York Public Library, Astor, Lenox, and Tilden Foundations. **195.** *Lycoris sprengeri: Curtis's Botanical Magazine* 123: t. 7547. (1897). **196.** Painting no. 476. *Male and female Trees of the Coco de Mer in Praslin.* Royal Botanic Gardens, Kew. Copyright © RBG Kew. **198,** Coco de mer by BGCI. **204.** Painting no. 475. *Male inflorescence and Ripe Nuts of the Coco de Mer, Seychelles.* Royal Botanic Gardens, Kew. Copyright © RBG Kew. **209.** Rosemary herb flowers © Marilyn Barbone / Dreamstime.com. **211.** Pressed flowers courtesy of enchantedgal-Stock (http://enchantedgal-stock.deviantart.com).

Every effort has been made to contact the appropriate copyright holders. The publisher would be happy to amend credit lines as necessary in subsequent printings.

Index

Page numbers in italics refer to illustrations and photographs.
A more comprehensive index is available at www.soniaday.com.

A NOTE ABOUT THE TYPE

The body of *The Untamed Garden* has been set in Filosofia, a typeface designed in 1996 by Zuzana Licko, co-founder of Émigré Fonts. The face is a modern interpretation of the classic Bodoni, allowing for applications that Bodoni's extreme contrasts cannot address, namely good readability in smaller text sizes.

BOOK DESIGN BY TERRI NIMMO